2009 Poetry Com

I have a dream 2009

Words to change the world

Martin Luther King

John Lennon

The Home Counties

Edited by Lisa Adlam

First published in Great Britain in 2009 by:

YoungWriters

Young Writers
Remus House
Coltsfoot Drive
Peterborough
PE2 9JX
Telephone: 01733 890066
Website: www.youngwriters.co.uk

Book Design by Spencer Hart & Tim Christian

SB ISBN 978-1-84924-509-8

Foreword

'I Have a Dream 2009' is a series of poetry collections written by 11 to 18-year-olds from schools and colleges across the UK and overseas. Pupils were invited to send us their poems using the theme 'I Have a Dream'. Selected entries range from dreams they've experienced to childhood fantasies of stardom and wealth, through to inspirational poems of their dreams for a better future and of people who have influenced and inspired their lives.

The series is a snapshot of who and what inspires, influences and enthuses young adults of today. It shows an insight into their hopes, dreams and aspirations of the future and displays how their dreams are an escape from the pressures of today's modern life. Young Writers are proud to present this anthology, which is truly inspired and sure to be an inspiration to all who read it.

For Nanny and Grandad
(go to page 170
16/12/09
Love Ryan

Contents

The Cornwallis Academy, Maidstone

The Hundred of Hoo School, Rochester

The Poems

I Have A Dream . . .

I have a dream
That one day I will be rich
And have a good man
Looking after me.

I have a dream
That all my worries and
Strife will disappear.

I have a dream
That I will become the
World's best beautician.

I have a dream
That my mum, dad and
Brother will reach
Everything they have ever
Wanted, as they're worth it.

I have a dream
That I have a big house
With an outside pool and a
Large decking area to chill.

I have a dream
That I have hot butlers
Serving me 24/7.

I have a dream
That everything is free
No more finance to pay
Or taxes to pay.

I have a dream
That there should be
No more school!
(Like that's going to happen!)

Charlotte Goddard (13)
Altwood CE Business & Enterprise College, Maidenhead

My Dream - The Dream I Always Dream

I have a dream . . .

I often dream this dream,
A dream so real to me,
I dream it could be a reality.

That one day there will be no war,
That we will unite as never before.

When people commit a crime,
The justice system would ensure that they do the time.
The hoodies, hooligans and thuggish behaviour,
Making us all feel a whole lot safer.

Teenage kids thinking they're cool,
Carrying knives on them, even at school.
Don't they realise carrying knives,
Is merely messing with people's lives?

This is my dream,
The dream I always dream.
I so badly want this dream to become a reality.

I really want my dream to last,
This way I know that poverty can be a thing of the past.

I dream this dream almost every night,
Hoping and praying for the world to unite.

Day by day nature's evolution
Is becoming full of pollution.
Scientists work hard for the conclusion,
But it's the people that have the solution.

I often dream this dream,
A dream so real to me,
I dream it will become a reality.

Robson Merritt (12)
Altwood CE Business & Enterprise College, Maidenhead

The Power Of Segregation

It's 1971
And my life is now a misery,
Segregation has taken over,
Life, power and death all over.
I have a dream
To make everything right,
To have world peace -
To stand and fight.
Now it's about colour and race,
It shouldn't matter;
We're all the same.
As we grow older
The force grows stronger.
I sit and wonder,
How much longer,
I can't stand and fight,
I'm black and proud.
But they won't accept me,
I'm out of their bounds!
I'm not with the group,
I'm not with the pack,
Just 'cause I'm different,
Just 'cause I'm black.
When will my nightmare come
To an end?
I'm scared to go out;
Or walk round the bend!
I've lost everything I have to be sure!
This really *is* the end,
I can't do it no more!

Abbie Kirk (14)
Altwood CE Business & Enterprise College, Maidenhead

I Have A Dream . . .

I have a dream that one day children in Africa will live in peace
And with all the benefits that I have lived with.
That one day they will have running water in their homes
And a warm, cosy bed that they can sleep in every night,
A dream so pure and kind-hearted, a dream . . .

I dream all their diseases could be cured and prevented,
And that they wouldn't have to live
Wondering if tomorrow they will die,
What kind of life is that?

I have a dream that the little children of Africa can have dreams
And goals in their lives and not just lie about having no dreams.
Of everything the children of Africa don't have,
A dream is one thing they should.

Hope. Courage. Determination for the future.
Dreams.

A dream is something people aspire to achieve,
And it's something that the children of Africa
Should be able to do.

I have a dream
That one day they can live in a warm house with heating.

I have a dream that six-year-old children don't have to
Look after their siblings because their mother has died.

I dream that they don't have to watch their mothers die.
I have a dream . . .
A dream that poverty will end . . .

Farrah Farhoudi (14)
Altwood CE Business & Enterprise College, Maidenhead

Let The Freedom Ring

I have a dream
That all will be well
That we will work in a team
That no child will cry or yell
Our dream is our theme
For all of our dreams.

Freedom is closed, not to be seen
Not to be heard or to be listened to
To only be thought about in silence
People dreamed as freedom flew
Freedom flew as people were hurt in violence
Freedom knew where it had been.

People would keep quiet
In all that they knew
Even if they were starved
And made to watch people eat stew
Treated as if they were carved
Then they had too much so they had a riot.

It lasted for days on end
So many got killed or hurt
No blood was meant to be spilt
They were all so very alert
The world just seemed to tilt
Then it was as if it had all been hemmed.

I have a dream . . .

Judith Mattock (13)
Altwood CE Business & Enterprise College, Maidenhead

I Have A Dream

Some people have dreams and make them come true
Others sit at home and wish they did too,
So be the first person and pursue your dream
Because things are never what they seem.

Martin Luther King wrote a speech
And lots of people he did teach
To treat people equally and just have fun
So everyone can sit and play in the sun.

Barack Obama became president
And his message was sent
That everyone's the same and can make history
Just believe and you will see.

Even pop stars were normal people like you
But they just did what they had to do.
And now their CDs are on the shelves
And all they did was believe in themselves.

So all I am saying is pursue your dream
Because things are never what they seem
You're either a person who makes your dreams come true
Or you sit at home and wish you did too.

Niall Billings (13)
Altwood CE Business & Enterprise College, Maidenhead

I Have A Dream!

I have a dream,
A dream where there is no more school,
We tell the teachers what to do
And they have to do what we say,
No more 'Tuck in your shirt!'
Or 'Where's your homework?'
That would be our job.

I have a dream,
A dream where we run our own school,
There are no more rules,
And we get to do what we want,
The teachers are children
And the children are teachers.

I have a dream
A dream where work is all the teachers do,
They work from dawn till dusk,
And we sit back and watch them,
No break, no lunch,
Just work, work, work.

I have a dream . . .

Thomas Haggarty (13)
Altwood CE Business & Enterprise College, Maidenhead

I Have A Dream . . .

I have a dream that knife crime stops,
We hear all the incidents of dying, it starts
Off teardrops.
When I'm walking the streets I see police taping
Things off saying 'Crime Scene'.
Blood, guts everywhere, it's the worst thing I've
Ever seen!
I have a dream that gun crime will stop.
You see the pictures with blood pouring out of
The top.
When I go to sleep, gunshots wake me up.
Guns are a threat, give me the till and shut
The hell up!
You only seem to care about these problems
When someone's died in your life
By drugs, guns or a knife.
So please stop coz I've already had enough
Strife.
I don't want these problems, I just want
Kids and a wife.

Kyle Dickens (14)
Altwood CE Business & Enterprise College, Maidenhead

I Have A Dream

I have a dream that I could be a millionaire
Help those who are needy, who need it the most.
I have a dream that money would grow on trees
So I could pick at it and pay off all my fees.

To help people's dreams come true.
To help them with their difficulties they may be going through.
I wish I could help those kids hungry and skinny
I feel sorry for them, so petite and mini.

If I had the money I would pay for children to go to school,
Just hoping they wouldn't take me for a fool.
Although I would help all those in need I would
Obviously keep some money to myself,
Maybe buy a brand new car, or a house
Even if it were for a little mouse.

After fulfilling my wide and wonderful dream,
I don't think it'll be as hard as it first did seem,
From helping, caring, sharing my ideas
I hope I will succeed without any fears.

Meera Ghedia (13)
Altwood CE Business & Enterprise College, Maidenhead

I Have A Dream . . .
That I'm Minted in Money

Wouldn't it be great to be minted in money,
Wouldn't it be great, wouldn't it be funny
To go out and buy whatever you want to,
To have a mansion and do what you want to do.

You wouldn't care if something got shattered,
You would go out and replace it
Like nothing else mattered.
Yeah, I have a dream.

I have a dream
That I could have an inside pool,
An inside gym,
I'd be so cool.

Wouldn't it be great to have a 100 inch screen,
Wouldn't that be great
Because they have never been seen.
This is the end and that's my dream.

Jordan Roberts (14)
Altwood CE Business & Enterprise College, Maidenhead

I Have A Dream . . .

I have a dream that one day poverty will end,
That people won't have to live in squalor
And people won't die of terrible illnesses
That can be cured.

I have a dream that people will appreciate what they have.
Society does not see what they have right in front of them,
They don't see how special their lives are
Compared to some people's.

I have a dream that one day those little children in Africa
Who have no hope
Will finally have their dream come true
And that they won't have to grow up alone and sad.

I have a dream that people will understand
What some people go through in life
And that they will have running water
And some proper food to get by on.

I have a dream that poverty will end.

Megan Millwater (14)
Altwood CE Business & Enterprise College, Maidenhead

I Have A Dream

I have a dream to be rich
Where I have a big swimming pool
That would be cool
I would be dancing like a fool

I have a dream that I will have some cats
I have a dream that I have lots of mats
I have a dream that I will get rats

I have a dream that I win a bet
That gets me out of debt
I have a dream to get a tea cup set
And a jumbo jet

I have a dream to skydive
I wish that I could drive
I have a dream to see a gig live
And to dance the jive

I hope this will happen.

Rochelle John (12)
Altwood CE Business & Enterprise College, Maidenhead

I Have A Dream

I have a dream that I will do well in school.
That I'll have a big house with an indoor pool,
I have a dream that I will go to university
And train to become a vet,
That I will have two horses and lots of pets.
I have a dream that I will live in the countryside,
That all day long all I have to do is ride.
I have a dream that I'll ride in the Olympics,
That I'll have a gorgeous thoroughbred with a tail that flicks.
I have a dream that there will be a cure for all illnesses,
That everyone will be happy,
And my life will be full of big surprises.

Jessica Hay (12)
Altwood CE Business & Enterprise College, Maidenhead

Strife Of A Chooser

Drugs cause violence
Gangs cause worse
It's like a curse.

People get killed
For not havin' money
Their blood is spilled
I just wanna tell you that
It isn't funny.

'Cos drugs come with more than
Just pleasure,
But debt
Blood
And the life of a loser
And strife of a chooser.

Jack Greenham (12)
Altwood CE Business & Enterprise College, Maidenhead

I Have A Dream . . .

I have a dream to make my family's deepest dreams come true,
And then go round the whole world helping people like you.

I have a dream to take care of all the different pets,
Then ask my dad what he wants and make sure that's what he gets.

I have a dream to be a pop star and have lots of money,
Then get married to David Beckham and call him my honey.

I have a dream that all the people who are not so well
Could feel better day by day and never go to Hell.

I have a dream that I could be popular at school,
And then make all the people think that I am really cool.

Dominika Krawczyk (12)
Altwood CE Business & Enterprise College, Maidenhead

The Spark In The Night

A light through the darkness
A spark in the night
A glimmer of hope through the fear and the fright.

A world full of hope
A world without fear
No time to worry about people held dear.

The lives that we lead
They all end the same
We end up alone, stone cold in a grave.

The end doesn't matter
It's the path that we take
And that all depends on the choices we make.

There is no change of path
The end just grows near
Second by second for the time that we're here.

Colour doesn't matter
Or race or religion
Everyone on Earth should have the same vision.

Some do not care
That bring death and destruction
That always leads to military functions.

The kindness and laughter
Will always come after
The pain and the sorrow that leads for tomorrow.

Many will say
That we should live today
But changing tomorrow can save ultimate sorrow.

Lives can be saved
If all make a stand
Make the place that we live a glorious land.

Aaron Rimmell (13)
Belhus Chase Humanities College, South Ockendon

I Dream

Everybody dreams once in a while,
Some can really hurt you, but some can make you smile.
Some dreams can be weird and some can be wonderful
But then you suddenly wake up and you can become tearful.

I dream of a future that I look forward to,
I reach all my goals and you reach yours too.
I dream I achieve medals of everyone's wonder,
While someone figures out how to solve world hunger.
I dream forever that my family will be by my side,
As I look to them, their eyes fill with pride.

I always dream of a fairytale ending,
But in the end, it's always my heart I'm defending
I dream of a happy place,
Where people hold each their hands as they say their grace.
I dream of a starry sky
Where I can wish that I could fly.

I dream of my dreams, nearly all the time,
All of my friends go together like lemon and lime,
I dream of a life that suits me the most
Where I am at friends' parties as the guest host.

I dream of an angel looking down on me,
Keeping me protected while I test curiosity.
But then I wake up feeling lucky and proud,
But my dreams will never be told, never be found,
They will never be said out loud.

Sophie Burroughs (14)
Belhus Chase Humanities College, South Ockendon

I Dream

I dream that one day I will see the adult world in my own eyes.

I feel that I will know myself like people know me
And to feel safe.

I dream that the whole world would be friendly
And we all can be trusted to love each other
And play with each other.

I dream that all people would stop worrying
And be calm like the ocean or the sea
And would not start to rage over small things.

I dream that I can sleep without worrying
That people will harm and kill.

I dream that you would dream the same dream I dream
So you can feel the pain that I share.

I dream that you would love and care
And don't feel restrained to a certain level.

I dream my heart has a reason to beat,
I dream that our hearts would meet.

I dream to dream and to believe
That the world is happy like me.

Cerrina Ball (14)
Belhus Chase Humanities College, South Ockendon

I Want To Be Famous!

F amous people inspire others to dream.
A nyone can be famous if they put their minds to it.
M any people dreamt about being famous and it happened.
O thers believe their dreams do not come true.
U sing your mind it may and will come true.
S ometimes people put their dreams at rest;
if you have, start them back up.

Georgie Phillips (12)
Belhus Chase Humanities College, South Ockendon

Change The World Today

Change the world
Would be a great thing
Change the world
Where everyone's clean.

Change the world
Where no racism is seen
Change the world
So people are not mean.

Change the world
Where people save lives
Change the world
Where no one has knives.

Change the world
Where colour or race is alright
Change the world
Where no one has a fight.

Change the world today
So we can all live in peace and quiet.

Matthew Hiam (13)
Belhus Chase Humanities College, South Ockendon

My Dream . . .

My dream is to save the world and save everyone in it,
I would make everyone fit and make them all feel special,
My dream would be to help the poor,
So they will not have to be hurt anymore,
My dream would be a special dream,
To make everyone feel good about how they seem,
My dream would be to make the world a better place,
And it would not matter about people's race,
My dream is what I want to be, a happy place indeed,
So poor people on this world wouldn't have to beg or plead.

Leanne Mann (12)
Belhus Chase Humanities College, South Ockendon

What If?

I have a dream, my dream is:
What if the world we live in was
A different place?
Or that we could have second chances.
What if the world was never polluted
Or poverty never existed?

What if the world never had child abuse
And children always felt safe?
What if racism never existed
And the world could be a happy place?
What if kidnappings never happened
And children stayed with parents?
What if worries had no meaning or a place in this world again?

What if this world never had unhappy lives
And every life story could have a happy ending?
What if having no money was never heard of?
Or the credit crunch never existed?
What if children being put into care was not an answer?
Life could always be so extravagant!

If only this world could exist and life could be like
A dream!

Sola Ajayi (11)
Belhus Chase Humanities College, South Ockendon

My Dream

M y dream is to rule the world
Y es, I know it's a lot, but I'd love it.

D reams can be amazing, only time will tell
R ight now, I have a big dream
E very dream will have a meaning
A ll the time, I believe in my dream
M aybe it will come true, who knows?

S ometimes, dreams do not come true
H ow will I know if I do not try?
A spiration
L ittle dreams can become big dreams
L ike mine has become today.

C haracteristics are a key to life
O nly you know what your dream is
M y dream is a *big* dream
E ver since I first dreamt of it, it's become bigger.

T iny dreams can lead to a big future
R ight now, I believe in my dream
U nderestimating others can affect their dream
E veryone can have a dream.

Matt Mason (13)
Belhus Chase Humanities College, South Ockendon

Inspired By A Dream

I paint pictures in my mind of how Britain should look
Then I open my eyes and reality hits,
Violence and crime put our country to shame.

My voice will be heard and inspire generations,
Such young and vulnerable people
Are being dragged into things that are hard to believe:
Drugs, alcohol, violence and sex
Are destroying Britain's reputation and ruining lives.

Parents are being put into situations
Where they are dreading
Letting their children out into the streets,
Therefore kids feel as if they are being wrapped in cotton wool.
If society doesn't change things will get worse.

Every voice should be heard
But people just brush things under the carpet
And pretend things will be OK
When we should be solving the problems
And not ignoring them.
I am inspired by a dream
And my dream will change the nation.

Lois Riley (13)
Belhus Chase Humanities College, South Ockendon

If Only . . .

If only the world was perfect,
What would life be about?
If only we never knew what poverty meant,
But that could only be dreamt.

If only the emotion hate did not even exist,
And war never broke out,
No countries would ever have to doubt.
If only racism was never heard of,
And everyone could just love.

If only everyone was just healthy,
And disease never was around.
If only there were no worries about global warming,
There would have to be no transforming.

If only the world was perfect,
What would life be about?
Not all is bad about the world,
But we can help change it
To make it the place I know it could be.

Shona Ross (14)
Belhus Chase Humanities College, South Ockendon

The World And I

I can dream that is true,
But I only dream of you,
My dreams can fill the sky,
But I wish people do not lie,
Oh the world will be so much better
If the world could come together,
Stop the wars in Iraq,
And keep people from attack,
People dying is so painful,
This makes the world look very shameful,
If we never knew what wars can do,
Maybe my dreams could come true,
In Flanders Fields crosses grow,
Between these poppies blow,
Everybody deserves a life,
Without living in a life of fright,
World peace could come true,
But this is all down to you.

Harry Jeacock (14)
Belhus Chase Humanities College, South Ockendon

Make The World A Better Place

We're living in a world full of violence and crime,
When all you worry about is money and time.
Parents worry about children getting hurt,
When they should be out playing in the dirt.
Children smoking, drinking and taking drugs,
Violence, criminals, arrogant thugs.

We're living in a world where there's different races,
But look around and they're all familiar faces.
Gangs are fighting, and people are dying.
Knife crime, shooting, bullets to the back,
We've got to say no, we've got to fight back.

Ashley Bedford (14)
Belhus Chase Humanities College, South Ockendon

My Dream Is?

My dream is to have an eco-friendly life for me and my family.

Young people don't have many lessons
On how to keep the world eco-friendly.

Do people know how to make an eco-friendly world
To lead to an eco-friendly life?

Red is the wrong choice but green is the right choice.
So we need everyone to represent the green not the red.

Everyone needs to take part in this so we can have a better life.

Also we need it to continue forever.

My dream is to have an eco-friendly life for me and my family.

I want you to take part and lead a happy life
For you and your family.

So we need to stop pollution.

Hollie Perkins (12)
Belhus Chase Humanities College, South Ockendon

The Modern Day Britain

Modern day Britain's getting harder by the minute,
Babies having babies and teenagers in the clinic.
Drunken sex and adultery to wives,
Innocent youths struggling to stay alive.

Zero percent regret to the heartache that is made,
It has become a regular thing when lives are lost by a blade.
Gang wars and riots are all over the news,
Instead of people helping they're putting across their views.

But in my heart there's hope for a better generation,
All we have to do is focus on education.
Britain *can* get better we all have to do our bit,
'Cause we're the ones that started it and now we finish it.

Jordy Mukeza (14)
Belhus Chase Humanities College, South Ockendon

The World And Me

When I dream, I dream of the world and me,
I dream of how the world used to be.
Maybe one day everyone would see
What we are doing to the world, just like me.

Violence is becoming a big issue, racism, drugs and murders,
It's all getting to me with a simple touch.
I watch the news and I'm seeing that it's all true,
Is it just me, or is it you too?

Parents don't like their kids going out and about,
They say it's for their safety, they say it's for their own good,
Sometimes they say scary things
Just to stop you from going about in the hood.

Sometimes I think I'm alone in this dark world,
But I know there are others around me that see what I see too,
Sometimes I think it's just the world against me.

Shannon Jervis (13)
Belhus Chase Humanities College, South Ockendon

I Have A Dream

I n the beginning we all have a dream but,

H ow it ends up is completely different.
A nd now we have to take action.
V ery big, or very small, stick to your dream
E ventually it could make a huge difference.

A lthough,

D reaming is dreaming and
R eality is reality.
E very day I think about my dream
A nd I think, is it possible to achieve?
M aybe.

Tysian Wood (14)
Belhus Chase Humanities College, South Ockendon

Imagine If

Imagine if the world was a better place
Full of joy and grace
No one cared about your hair, your eyes, your face.

The world would be a better place.

Imagine if people didn't like you because of the way you look
Then people should turn around and look at themselves.
No one is perfect. Everyone is different.

People should like you for who you are not what you look like.

Imagine if the world was a better place
Not filled with a crime case . . .
And everyone brought peace and respect around this place.

People shouldn't be bad and do crimes, it gets them nowhere,
In life they do deserve to have one,
They're just not choosing that option.

Natasha Smith (12)
Belhus Chase Humanities College, South Ockendon

I Have a Dream

I have a dream to sail the sea to see pirates,
People say I'm different in every single way,
But then again no one wants to be the same.
Also people say you should do this, you do that
But I like the way I am.
So I will put my hair down and live again,
Have some dignity and be brave
And let people and children drive at every age.

Shannon Walker (12)
Belhus Chase Humanities College, South Ockendon

A Different World

I have a dream of a different world
Where everyone's all the same and they don't have to hide
Behind layers of make-up to be liked by their friends.

I have a dream of a different world
Where children could live in a worry-free environment
And be happy, and feel loved with a supportive family
And friends that care.

I have a dream of a different world
Where animals weren't killed for their fur
Or abused by their owners.

I have a dream of a different world
Where every person had proper food and water
And good living conditions and medical care.

I have a dream of a different world.

Alexzandra Stokes (12)
Belhus Chase Humanities College, South Ockendon

I Want A World

I want a world full of freedom and peace
A world full of happiness and no grief.

I want a world full of care
Just like a big cuddly bear.

I want a world full of love
Where anybody can have a hug.

I want a world where anybody can be free
And buzz around like a careless bee.

I want a world where poverty can't hear
And poverty can never come near.

I want a world and you want it too
We can all do it together we can all do.

Abigail Aladenika (12)
Belhus Chase Humanities College, South Ockendon

My Dream Is Big!

M y dream is a big one
Y our dream might be the same

D reams can be enthralling, some dreams can be sad
R eally a dream can be anything
E veryone will have one
A lot will be the same
M y dream is a changing one

I dream for a peaceful world
S ome may somewhat disagree

B ut I feel very strongly
I know what I want to change
G reed and violence should be no more

And then we can all see that my dream is not so big.

Jordan Blake (14)
Belhus Chase Humanities College, South Ockendon

A Dream I Have!

A dream I have should inspire the world,
A place that's disease free,
A place where there's no poverty,

A dream I have should inspire the world,
A place that emotions don't rule,
A place people want to be,

A dream I have should inspire the world,
A place for peace and no animal cruelty,
A place for the rich and poor,

A dream I have should inspire the world,
A place we love,
A place we share,

A dream I have *needs* to inspire the world!

Beth Fisk (11)
Belhus Chase Humanities College, South Ockendon

Sometimes

Sometimes . . .
I can't help but to imagine
What life would be like if the world was perfect,
No poverty, no crime, no violence, but respect.
A world where everything was done to perfection
Filled with nothing but affection.

Sometimes . . .
I can't help but to imagine
What life would be like if there was peace,
No war and weapons
And people's bodies lying on the floor in pieces,
No fear but safety, nothing but equality.
Would that time ever come
When everyone would feel worth an important quality?

Oluwatosin Omotosho (13)
Belhus Chase Humanities College, South Ockendon

I Have A Dream . . .

I have a dream, one day people will realise how
Much they are putting our Earth in danger
With global warming.

If we don't stop now, we are putting us all in danger.
The danger of flooding us all.
The danger of flooding us
All.

We are also putting the animals' lives at risk,
Such as the polar bears and the penguins.

We can stop this if we are all in this together!

Save our world,
Stop global warming!

Megan McIntyre (11)
Chase High School, Westcliff-on-Sea

I Have a Dream . . .

I have a dream, a dream deep
Inside my heart, it's personal
To me and it's not to be seen
Apart from today when
I hope it's displayed and
Is ready to come true so I can
Help this world.
I have a dream
A dream to fulfil.

My dream is to go to Africa
To save the animals, to save the
People who live there, the people
Who see their country, their world
Quickly vanishing.
I have a dream
A wonderful dream.

To help life for others is helping your
Own, this world can shine, I know it
Can, let's come together as a team, now it's
Time, it's time to change.

I have a dream to stop hate and
Spitefulness, a dream to stop
Tears from having to fall, a
Dream to stop pain and hurt.
To stop human hate.
I have a dream, a dream to stop hate.

Courtney Webb (11)
Chase High School, Westcliff-on-Sea

I Have A Dream . . .

I have a dream . . .
No polluting our planet
No noise pollution
No dumping things into rivers
No destroying our planet . . .

I have a dream . . .
No animals being threatened
No poachers
No hunters
No cruelty to animals . . .

I have a dream . . .
No deaths in third world countries
No homeless people
No neglected children
Equal rights to everyone . . .

I have a dream . . .
No bullies
No terrorists
No murders
No crime
These are my dreams
If only they'd come true . . .

Sean Farrugia (12)
Chase High School, Westcliff-on-Sea

I Have A Dream . . .

Child abuse will stop,
Children are dying,
Their parents are beating them,
What have the children done?
They're innocent.

Animals are beaten,
They should be cared for,
Not beaten till death,
People go to jail,
It hurts the animals.

Children in Africa are dying,
They're dying every thirty seconds,
It's not a very safe place to live,
It has disease,
They don't have any clean water.

Bullying is horrible,
What have they ever done to you?
Why do you bully them?
Black or white,
Disabled or ugly,
Or do you just not like them?

Abigail Eastwick (11)
Chase High School, Westcliff-on-Sea

I Have A Dream . . .

I have a dream that
One day global warming
Would stop polluting the
Planet then the planet would
Be a better and safer place.

I have a dream that every
Living animal would be safe,
We make coats and handbags
Out of animals, it is cruelty,
People should let nature take its course.

I also have another dream
About the homeless,
We spend money on things
We don't need, sweets or clothes
And more but we could
Give that little extra bit of
Money to the homeless people
Be kind and do something
Good in your life!

I have a lot of dreams and I hope
At least one of these dreams would come true.

Chloe Thwaites (12)
Chase High School, Westcliff-on-Sea

I Have A Dream . . .

I have a dream of perfect harmony,
No fighting and no war,
No pollution and no poverty,
What a better world it would be.

I have a dream of no bullying,
No disagreement and no tears,
No harm or hurtfulness,
What a better world it would be.

I have a dream of good emotions,
No Pandora's box and no bad feelings,
No badness or worry,
What a better world it would be.

I have a dream of agreement,
No arguments and no anger,
We should have more patience and more understanding,
What a better world it would be.

The world would be perfect, a better place for everyone,
But will my dream come true?

That was my dream.
What about yours?

Victoria Champion (12)
Chase High School, Westcliff-on-Sea

I Have A Dream

My dream, a dream that will change the world,
No poverty, unemployment or homelessness,

Would make a better place,
I'm sure,

Maybe someday it will happen,
But then,
Wouldn't the world just be 'too perfect'?

How I wonder
If all the hate and bad things will ever end.

But it probably won't,
And that is why people dream,

Dream of making a better world,
Somewhere we feel safe,

Just listen to my dream
Hear me say,

That I want poverty to stop,

One day.

Eden Caceres-Jimenez (12)
Chase High School, Westcliff-on-Sea

World Hunger

Imagine . . .
All those mothers,
Their children barely
Reach the age of 5
Only because they have no
Clean water.

If a country has a doctor,
Most people can't afford it,
We can help them,
Can't we!

Everything deserves a chance to live
For whom they are,
Not what people
Want them to be.

One day,
One dream,
All of these will
Come true.

Chelsea Springate (12)
Chase High School, Westcliff-on-Sea

I Have A Dream . . .

I have a dream . . . that we would live in harmony,
Together at peace, not at war,
We shouldn't take the world for granted,
And be grateful for what we have.
Walk to school or take the bike,
Forget about cars and buses.

I have a dream . . . that animals would be free,
Endangered animals are becoming extinct,
For fur and meat, not the respect they need,
They may not be human,
They may not be our pets,
Treat them fairly, how they deserve to be treated.

I have a dream . . . that criminals would stop!
To make the world a happy and safe place,
No more hurting and no more stealing,
And treat others the way you would like to be treated.
We should make the world a happy place,
Everyone would be happier, don't you think?

Thahura Miah (11)
Chase High School, Westcliff-on-Sea

I Have A Dream . . .

I have a dream
That one day crime would stop,
That everyone were friends
And didn't steal from shops.

I have a dream
That nobody would kill,
And that they realise
How their families must feel.

Vandalism, mugging and terrorism too,
Such awful things that
Nobody
Should do.

Everyone's had enough of this awful behaviour,
So stop crime today,
And do us all a favour!

Brooke Stevens (12)
Chase High School, Westcliff-on-Sea

I Have A Dream . . .

I have a dream . . .
A dream that one day the world will change,
We would live in nice tidy streets,
And everyone would have somewhere to live,
So they don't have to live on the main roads or alleyways,
And everyone will have enough money to buy food and drink,
And everyone will be able to hear, speak and see,
So they can have proper conversations with people.

But that is not the end,
Every time I walk down the street
And I see these people,
Whether it's tramps begging for money
Or deaf and dumb people needing help,
Or even blind and disabled people
Struggling to live,
I dream that they can live their life like a normal person,
Speak, hear, see and walk . . . and even think.

Jack Norton (12)
Chase High School, Westcliff-on-Sea

I Have A Dream . . .

I have a dream that one day
There will be no more wars.

I have a dream there will be no more wars,
No more hunting animals,
No more stabbings,
No more drugs,
No more cigarettes,
No more crimes,
No more diseases.

That is my
Dream.

Michael Stains (12)
Chase High School, Westcliff-on-Sea

I Have A Dream . . .

I have a dream . . .
That someday people would
Stop polluting the Earth.
My reasons are simple,
As the heat is rising
All the animals that live in cold places will be killed off,
Because all the ice is melting from the heat.

I have a dream . . .
That someday the world will be rid
Of all the silly teenagers that go around killing innocent people, It's just not nice.
And all the bad people that do nasty things to children
And take them away from their families.
I feel so sorry for the families
That have to live knowing their child is missing.

Maisie Perry (11)
Chase High School, Westcliff-on-Sea

Imagine

Imagine
A world with no flowers,
Imagine
A world with no bees,
Imagine
A world with more pollution,
Imagine
A world with nobody there,
Imagine
No voice in the rustle,
Imagine
No one will like this world,
Imagine.

Abigail Chapman (12)
Collingwood College, Camberley

Imagine, Imagine, Imagine

Imagine
A world with no pollution and no diseases,
Imagine
Winning the lottery; being a football player,
Imagine
Being rich and famous,
Imagine
A world made of chocolate; living in a tree house.

Imagine
No crimes, no animals and no laws,
Imagine
No gravity, no sun and no roads,
Imagine
You are the light in the world,
Imagine
You are the only boy,
Imagine
You are the only girl.

Imagine
No toys and no playing
Imagine
No grass, no mud and no floor,
Imagine
You are an animal, an ant, a bird or a fish,
Imagine
If you were poor on the street, on the floor.

Joshua Payne (12)
Collingwood College, Camberley

No School, No Life

Imagine
If no one had to go to school
Children would be happier
Laughing and playing
With all their friends.

Imagine
All the people without a home
Living on the street
No education, job, food or life
Struggling to live another day.

Imagine
All the children that will never be happy
All the people that die of hunger
People suffering and crying
Huddling together to stay warm.

So maybe school is not so bad
To get an education
A job, money, food and clothes.
So be grateful for school,
Or live a painful life.

Jack Tilley (13)
Collingwood College, Camberley

Imagine

Imagine
If no one died,
Imagine
If we lost no lives,
Imagine
If there was no pollution,
Imagine
If there was a world revolution,
Imagine
If there was no harm in the world,
Imagine
If we all had diamonds and pearls,
Imagine
If no one was bad,
Imagine
If no one was sad,
Imagine
Imagine
Imagine.

Amy Shepherd (12)
Collingwood College, Camberley

Paradise

Imagine
A world with no racism
Imagine
A world with no fighting
Imagine
A world with no discrimination
Imagine
A world with no criminals
Imagine
Paradise!

Macauley Green (13)
Collingwood College, Camberley

I Have A Dream

I have a dream
That I'll touch the sky
I have a dream
That I'll fly high.

I have a dream
That I will soon find love
I have a dream
To fly like a dove.

I have a dream
We will always be friends
I have a dream
We'll make it through the bends.

I have a dream
That I will be glowin'
I have a dream
That I'll win the contest
For this poem.

Farayi Msipha (12)
Collingwood College, Camberley

My World

A world without grief
B ecause I want a world that's happy
B ecause I want a world where everyone is happy
I want a world without racism
E xtinguish the people who are racists
S aving all the people that are dying

D ifferences should not be made
R eligions should all be the same
E very country should be friends
A rmies should all be friends
M y world would be so cool.

Abbie Weaver (12)
Collingwood College, Camberley

I Have A Dream

I have a dream
That one day this world will be in
Peace
Harmony
Love.

I have a dream
That all children will have
A warm bed
Fresh water
Warm food.

I have a dream
That everyone will have
Medical care
Healthy life
Happy life.

Just imagine!

Kevin Heath (13)
Collingwood College, Camberley

I Have A Dream

I llnesses,

H omelessness,
A buse
V ictimisation,
E verybody's got a family,

A nybody can get a job,

D isabilities,
R ioting,
E verybody has money,
A nger,
M ake a difference.

David Caddick (12)
Collingwood College, Camberley

From Violence Into Silence

I have a dream of peace,
No fighting and no war,
To stop the hurtful suffering,
Peace for evermore.

To love and cherish your neighbour,
To forgive and forget the past,
To help and respect the different,
To make this world-love last.

Try to look beyond the hatred,
Try to look ahead and see
The value of world peace and love,
What a great world this could be!

Destroy the hate inside you,
Make an end to all the fear,
Turn violence into silence,
Make it disappear.

Amy Richards (13)
Collingwood College, Camberley

My Dream

I have a dream that a light will lead in the dark,

H ate will be a thing of the past.
A nyone and everyone will be treated as an equal,
V enomous remarks will be forgotten.
E veryone will be loved as a brother or sister,

A nyone can call anywhere home.

D eath and destruction will be in history,
R acism will never be used again.
E very opportunity is open to everyone,
A nger is controlled and not used to strike.
M aybe this will all happen.

Jake Whittaker (13)
Collingwood College, Camberley

Imagine

Imagine
If you could fly,
Imagine
If no one could cry,
Imagine
A summer as a summer,
Imagine
The sun shining high,
Imagine
The world full of rubbish,
Imagine
A place like a dream,
Imagine
The whole world eating cream,
Imagine
Just imagine,
Just imagine.

Samantha Warren (11)
Collingwood College, Camberley

Imagine

Imagine
That no man would die,
Go up in the sky
Look down below,
Never go back,
Stuck in that gap,
Imagine staying alive forever and ever,
Stay alive as long as a feather,
People were healthy, and never got ill,
No need to take that 'good for you' pill,
Imagine.

Lily Dawson (12)
Collingwood College, Camberley

Dreams, That's All We Have

My past is my past
And I don't want to share,
Why should I?
It is mine.

My future is mine
And it will never come,
For the future is never now.

Now, that is what's real,
Now never passes,
It is always now.

Dreams, that's all we have,
Dreams for a future that will never come,
Memories of a past, good or bad,
Dreams, that's all we have.

Angelique Derman (13)
Collingwood College, Camberley

Imagine

Imagine
No fighting for tomorrow,
Imagine
No discrimination,
Imagine
No child suffering,
Imagine
No child dies tomorrow,
Imagine
Every day is a good day,
Imagine
My good day will last forever,
Imagine.

Chelsea Sears (12)
Collingwood College, Camberley

Making A Difference

Imagine
One person, one voice, one difference,
Imagine
One voice making history,
Imagine
Going down in history, being known,
Imagine
Being the voice that makes someone else's life different,
Imagine
Making the world a better place for everyone,
Imagine
If you were the one who made poverty history,
Imagine
What could you do?
Imagine!

Kirsty Britten (13)
Collingwood College, Camberley

Imagine

Imagine
No pollution,
Imagine
A world without homework,
Imagine
A school made of chocolate,
Imagine
A school run by children,
Imagine billions of things.

Matthew Fairman (12)
Collingwood College, Camberley

Imagine

Imagine
Ruining the planet and killing everyone.
Imagine
No pollution.
Imagine
No diseases.
Imagine
No one would die young. People would live a full life.
Imagine
No crime.
Imagine
Nobody would steal or murder.
Imagine
No one feeling stupid or less than the person next to them.
Imagine this.

Barry Clark (12)
Collingwood College, Camberley

Imagine

I n the world there should be peace,
M ight there be in the future?
A nd we can live in harmony if there is,
G ive people a chance to explain,
I n the future.
N ever be a killer and
E nter a world of peace.

Ben Garrett (13)
Collingwood College, Camberley

The Boy With A Dream

There once was a boy who was different.
He was badly abused but defiant.
His views defined,
He spoke his mind
And now this boy's not so different.

This boy who is now not so different,
He hated the world, it was wrong.
He changed the world,
His views they curled
What the world's views were like.

He had a dream and so can you.
One person *can* change the world,
And you know it.
So make an effort to make someone's life better.

Darren Finch (12)
Collingwood College, Camberley

I Have A Dream

I have a dream . . .
To make this blue and green planet a better place.
Lots of people have dreams and talents that they never fulfil,
Hidden away, scared of how people will judge them.
Stop cruelty to animals and children,
Make peace with other countries,
And never forget those people
Who've sacrificed their lives for us.
Never give up on your dream.

Grace Hardy (12)
East Court School for Dyslexia, Ramsgate

I Have A Dream

I have a dream about light and love
Light and love is beautiful
Helpful
Racism is not nice
People in Africa need more help and food
Fresh water is needed in most parts of the country
Help the penguins in the Antarctic because of the global warming
Family is the best to stay with you.

Antonio Sales (12)
Harbour School, Dover

I Have A Dream

C hildren need care
H elp them to live
I magination, wow!
L ovely laughter
D elighted to play
R unning away from monsters
E xcited to see you
N ever ignore them.

Callum Butcher (12)
Harbour School, Dover

Love For Dean Luckhurst

I see your eyes wherever you go
Under the love sky I touch your heart with dreams
I like the way you look every day
You are sweet as a flower
You are as cute as the sun in your eyes
I think you are totally loving.

Lucy Kneeshaw (12)
Harbour School, Dover

Monster!

When I walked in the room there he was
Standing in front of her with a
Look of rage mixed with happiness for hurting
Her.
She was scared, tears pouring from her eyes.
Then he snapped his head round to glare at me.

He'd yell and raise his fist and smash glasses
When she tried to help me, he would hit
And hit her hard
She'd fall to her knees and would laugh
And come closer to me
Then with a horrifying look he'd explode
Like a bomb
And smack me and push me to my room.

There I would sit in the corner like a
Little baby
Not wanting to move or go out there to
The sadness
Emotional and physical abuse that awaits
Me
I was afraid for not only myself but
My mum as well
I hate it when she cries or is in pain
He is a *Monster!*
I would say to myself over and over
I long for the day it's over
I'm free of the forcefulness and terrible
Aggression that fills the household
Maybe that day would come and it could be
Just me and Mum.

I wish I could run away!

It's morning now and time to rise
I hate the look of Mum in the morning
Bruises all over her body
I stumble to the door still with the
Broken toe I gained last week
When I'm out of my only sanctuary

The house seems so different
Curtains are open, letting the sun shine in
I make it to my mum's room hoping
She's not depressed
There she is on her bed; not looking
Dead
Since she married that *Monster*
Her spirit has died
But she looks alive
I clamber up on the bed then she tells
Me the *Monster* has left!

This day has come
I'm overjoyed with passion
And happiness
We can talk and not have to worry
Anymore.
I can finally move on and
Make friends
And no more secrets!

Now I'm free to be
Me!

I love you Mama!

Cassandra Hyett (12)
Hextable School, Swanley

Bullies

I'm sitting hereon my own
Hating myself being alone
When it happens no one seems to care
I hate it, it's just not fair
People hurting me, making me cry
When it comes to confess, I have to lie
Bullies make me feel I'm small
I want to be someone who's pride is tall.

Reuben Rohard (11)
Hextable School, Swanley

No Answers

As I lay silently in a dark
Empty house thinking how was
I going to get through
Tomorrow, drowning in my own
Sorrow.

My head was filling with
Questions, how? When? And
Why was this happening
To me? But I could find
No answers.

But all of a sudden I heard
The front door open; then
I heard it slamming back
Shut, I could hear footsteps
Stomping up the stairs
It was my mum, then she
Suddenly burst into my room.

She was reeking of wine
Smoke and beer
Right now I just wished I wasn't here
She turned on my light
Her face full of rage
I had nowhere to hide
I was trapped in this cage.

But even though she made
Me lonely and sad she
Was still my hero because
She was the only one I've ever had.

She looked at me in disgust
But all I wanted was
For her to love me.
As she left the room
My eyes started to fill
With tears of pain, she did
Not hurt me physically but her
Look told me all.

I cried myself to sleep
But from my mum that night I no longer heard a peep
I was left thinking
Wasn't every child supposed
To have a mum and dad
That loved them?

But tomorrow none of
This would matter
Because tomorrow I was
Going to see my dad for
The first time . . . ever!

The next morning I woke
Up full of hope and joy
Was it going to go well
Or all end in tears?

Sophie James (12)
Hextable School, Swanley

Heart Of War

War is a bad thing
Terrorists aren't a good thing
I never knew what war was for
But now I do
It's so a crazy man doesn't rule the world
Even though he'd like to
He might do it for a change
But if he is
He could work with us
Not bomb us
War is like a time bomb
People miss birthdays
Fun with family
And Christmas
As war rages on
I wish I could diffuse the time bomb.

Ross Goodall (13)
Hextable School, Swanley

Suffering Of A Child

Why did they do this to me?
Why did they always kick and punch?
When I didn't know what I had done.

They kicked me on the staircase
On my way to bed
They punched me in the bathroom
When I brushed my teeth
And beat me up when I was asleep.

The suffering they caused me
All the hurt and pain
The people I called Mum and Dad
Have beaten me again.

I couldn't go to school
Because of my bruises
I couldn't go out in case I told a soul
I didn't want to live
But I didn't want to die.

I never really had a name
My parents just used to scream
'Girl get here!'
Then they'd beat me with whatever they could find.

I never used to cry
I never used to plead
I knew it wouldn't work
When they were in their drunken state.

I had waited for the day that I would be free
Since the day I was born
Now that day has come
I'm now sixteen
I'm going to school
And when I look back
I don't feel dread
I don't feel pain
All I feel is stronger and I feel relief
But all I know is that I will never treat a child like that.

The confusion and pain
The hurt and isolation
Their fiery fists of fury
Punching here and there
There's no need for the red blood of a child
To shed in to the air
For they have done nothing
But the parent is all to blame
Drinks and booze all day long
Making them like a fire in a wooden city
Burning everything in its path
Burning buildings everywhere
Not caring who it hurts.

It has to end!
It has to stop!

Eden Palmer (12)
Hextable School, Swanley

Birthdays

Birthdays only come once a year
I guess mine is quite near

Sweets, jelly and a Chelsea bun
Lots of children having fun
Bouncy castle, running around
Maybe a magician or clown.

Birthday cakes are the main tradition
Eating out if it's nice weather conditions
Party hats and lots of cheers
Even some happy tears.

Enjoy the time you have when you're a child
Before you're old and in the wild
But always remember to make a wish
You don't want to be a cold fish.

Jennifer Kemp (13)
Hextable School, Swanley

Me And My Friend's Dream

I know this girl
She's my best friend
She is cool and friendly
She always sets her own trend.

Her name is Keisha
She is 12 years old
She lives next to me in London
We are always cold.

We may not be sisters
Keisha and me
But we're both the same
We act like family.

She tells me jokes
Funny and bad
But when she tells me secrets
I feel sorry and sad.

The secrets she tells me
Are about family and friends
About alcohol and abuse
It's upset the message she sends.

Keisha's dad is an alcoholic
And her mum's an abuser
They treat her like dirt
And that doesn't amuse her.

Her dad just gulps
Sitting down on his chair
And her mum just puffs
Before she begins to swear.

When Keisha's at home
She goes straight to her room
She cries and quivers
Until she hears a boom.

When she runs downstairs
She finds a broken bottle of whisky
She grabs her phone and a bag
And she doesn't forget her house key.

When Keisha calls me
She says, 'Can we meet somewhere?'
I say, 'OK, where?'
She then replies, 'I don't really care!'

Keisha tells me what happens
I say that it will be OK
But when she looks at me
She says, 'I want to run away!'

Me and Keisha have a dream
That her mum and dad would stop
If they did, they'd be a family
And for both if us it would be a cherry on the top.

Chanelle Camilleri (12)
Hextable School, Swanley

They Don't Care

Here I stand on my own because no one likes me
I feel sad, I feel hurt because the things they say
Are nasty
I need to tell, I need to tell but I'm scared they won't
Believe me
Their iron fists in my face, I can't look at myself no more.

I need to know if someone can help me, I've asked but
No one cares about me
A bit of hope will be lovely,
I've got to be strong maybe.

Inside I feel lonely but I've got to stand up
And be a bigger person
Now I'm strong I feel better, I've got to tell now
Now I've told I can make myself a better person.

Joe Kular (11)
Hextable School, Swanley

One Big . . .

Secrets
Lies
Deceitful
The way she keeps it inside.

Acting
Pretending
Deceiving
She pretends she's done nothing wrong.

I've caught her
Many, many times before
I don't know what to do
To talk to her or not.

My sister
She's seen her. She came to me
I told her no, of course not.
Whether she believed me, I don't know.

Her breath smells like a fire
Burning away
Face full of lies
With every word she says.

She is a giant one
It really is harmful
Eating her liver
Cigarette!

She is like a burning fire
Always has a short fuse
Taking it out on me
I haven't done anything.

I hate it when she lies
I never do
It really upsets me
To see her like this.

She doesn't know I know
I don't know what to do
Tell my dad
Or not.

I hope she gets found out
Or even better tell
So that this way
She isn't one big *cigarette!*

Shannon Keys (13)
Hextable School, Swanley

Paradise

BBQ, picnic
Blue sea, white sand
Palm trees, peace
Hammock, swaying
Calm.

Chantelle Wheeler (13)
Hextable School, Swanley

My Island

Smell of coconuts
Sea smashing, rushing
Sand running through your fingers
And the trees sway in the wind.

Sean Pilfold (13)
Hextable School, Swanley

Violence In Silence

Anger, depression, sadness
As I walk through the door
Pressure, pain, grief
While she's lying on the floor
Excitement, relief, joy
When my dad walks in
Outrage, disgust, obstruction
When he kicks her in the shins.

Daydreaming out the window
Just starting to drool
Hoping Mum will be alive
When I come home from school
Then I hear the bell go
And rush to pack my bag
So I can run home really fast
To check if she's alright.

I'm running like the wind
To make sure that she's fine
But when I get to our house . . .

'I've kicked dad out!'
She yelled at me
Her smile so big with glee
And since then, me and Mom
Live in total harmony!

Ella Hargittai (11)
Hextable School, Swanley

My Football Dream - Haiku

Cheering, roaring, clap
Ball, water, goalpost, gloves, grass
Chicken pies, air, tea.

Harry Phillips (12)
Hextable School, Swanley

Bullies In The School Yard

When I went to school one day
I went on the computer and shouted, 'Hooray!'
But something made me stop
It was the old school bully Tommy Pop
Somehow I didn't like him
And he hated me and Kim.

He used to like me
Now I have to hide up a tree
I felt isolated and neglected
I felt disgruntled and rejected
I had to tell someone about it
Not someone who steals my PE kit.

One day I told my mum
That Tommy had broke my drum
I felt angry and unhappy
Depressed and snappy
I said, 'What the hey
I'm going to do it my way.'

Went into school after my little talk
And having a calming walk
I knew what I was going to say
Something to brighten up my day
I ran as fast as a cheetah
Hoping he wasn't holding a beater.

Something then felt good
As it always should
I went up to him and said, 'Stop
No more Tommy Pop.'
He listened well and ran away
That's my poem on this fine day.

Max Swaisland (12)
Hextable School, Swanley

My Past

One loud scream
As I saw my sister run downstairs
Her face white as snow
She hesitated as her pale face told me what
I needed to know

My window! My window!
I saw a dark shadow
The shadow of a face we dread to see
He really hurt my family and me

My hurtful past
I'm glad it didn't last
That day I came back from school
The tears on my mum's face
The room so very cool
As my mum turned to me, her face red
'I'm sorry girls, your uncle is dead.'

Her best friend, her brother
He was the only one there for my mother
With him not here
We knew we'd have to live with this fear

Every day we lived and breathed
This horrible man was hurting my mum, my sister and me

But every cloud has a silver lining
And after all that happened, I'm still shining!
The horrible man is under lock and key
And life is better for my family and me.

Katrina Bailey (13)
Hextable School, Swanley

My Dad!

Everyone is in deep depression
And has a sad, upset expression
If only
I wasn't so lonely
I am in so much pain
I can't explain.

I feel really sad
Mum says it is so bad
I'm horrified
My dad had died
My mum is so scared
But she is still strong and prepared.

My eyes have tears leaking out
I'll never stop crying, I doubt
Forever frightened
As the day brightened
I started to see
That worries don't worry me.

I haven't forgotten my dad
And I still get sad
But not all the time
Even though he committed an evil crime
I really, really miss him
I even made him a Sim.

Me and him together
If only forever!

Brooke Connor (11)
Hextable School, Swanley

When I Come Home

When I come home and open the door
All I see is you, drunk on the floor
No time to play
No time for me in the day
First I make tea
Then I change the nappy on the baby
I sigh off to bed with my inner pain
Thinking tomorrow's another day; I don't want to do it again

Three o'clock in the morning
You wake me with your roaring
You're as loud as a lion
I listen to you hitting my brother Ryan
Oh no, you're coming in here
I can already smell the stench of beer
Your lightning fists impact on my bones
All you can hear are my horrific groans

As you leave me weeping in my bed
Think of Dad, the last words he said
'I'm here if you need me, I can turn things around'
I climb out the window and fall to the ground
Sneaking a long way from that house
So quiet I'm just like a mouse

Now I found refuge to save me from that place
Dad's plan of action is to overcome Mum's drinking case
Now my wounds have healed
I'm glad it's all ended.

Christopher Herbert (12)
Hextable School, Swanley

Daddy

I have only a brother
And my mother
But then there's also my dad
He gets angry and makes us sad
He likes drinking and smoking
When he's around no one's joking.

As I try to go to sleep at night
He wakes me up with quite a fright
As he hits my mum with his stone fist
So many more things I could list
He hits her hard and powerful
Marrying him, she's a fool.

We have to get out of here
I cannot bear to shed just one more tear
At my birthday our eyes meet
Dare I ask for a birthday treat?
I look at his hard, angry face and think
He looks like a statue, this must link
To his next move, what have I done?
I know already this won't be fun.

I look at him for the last time ever
Oh mum had been so clever
No more attacks
He's never coming back
She went to the police while he was sleeping
Now there won't be any more weeping.

Rachel Sutton (12)
Hextable School, Swanley

Jade Goody

She will always be know as
Jolly Jade
She was happy although she
Had to change the boy's nappies
She had such a nice
Wedding although she knew
She wasn't gonna stay
She had such nice ways
Especially on bad days
What she did to help the boys
Wasn't just silly toys
She knew that it was time
To go although she couldn't
Let go
At least we know what
She wanted to do is done
She has now had to let go
We said what we wanted to
Say
We're not all happy that
She couldn't stay but that's
The way
We said goodbye
And that's all we can say.

Ellie Thornton (12)
Hextable School, Swanley

Dreaming

Dreaming
Is for anyone
Dreaming
Is for you
Dreaming
Can be a lot of fun
Dreaming
Has a lot in store
Dreaming
Takes you far away
Dreaming
Of places you would like to stay
Dreaming
Is like a friend
Dreaming
Can be bad like nightmares
Dreaming
Is coming to an end
Dreaming
Should never end

I dream for peace
I dream for no diseases
I dream for everyone to be happy.

Scott Swift (13)
Hextable School, Swanley

Bullying Is A Disgrace

B ullying is a disgrace
U nhappiness on someone's face
L et the world be kind
L et bullying be refined
Y ou can stand up to these monsters
I f you try you'll find the right answers
N o one should ever be a bully
G etting what you want is selfish truly.

I nside you feel as if your tummy is tight
S cared, alone, filled with fright.

A lways leaving what happens inside

D oing nothing to help it
I f you tell someone now
S omething will come around
G ood, great, graceful feelings
R unning away has now turned to healing
A way goes grief
C rawling out from underneath
E veryone, stand up and say, till all the bullies go away

Now inside you feel like a rainbow
As happy as a clown, you will never be sad again.

Abigail Johnson (12)
Hextable School, Swanley

Cookie Island

Mixed dough, warmth of sun
Big huge waves hitting the ground
Cookies crumble all around.

Ryan Fowler (13)
Hextable School, Swanley

I'm Scared

I lay at night and hold my teddy tight
Mummy and Daddy are downstairs
They sound like big grizzly bears
I hold my ears
But I still have great fear
Why is this happening to me?
It feels like my heart's been stung by a big bee
But no, it's just my feelings
To be honest I would rather be bleeding
They need some help
Or this family is going to melt
When I'm at school I'm not too shy
But when I'm at home I feel like I have to hide
I act like myself
But feel like a doll on a shelf
I want to be free
I just want to be me
Inside I feel lonely
So I just dream of ponies
It's been two weeks
Mummy and Daddy are happy
So I don't have to stay with my nanny.

Katie Durant (11)
Hextable School, Swanley

Liverpool Dream

Cheering, roaring, mud in my mouth
As the ball sails in the box
A roaring crowd shouts in excitement.

Ryan Russel (13)
Hextable School, Swanley

Death But Life

Death
Is commonly feared
Death
Will always come
Death
Will have to come.

But
For time to come we are free
But
Sometime we will see
But
It will come for us.

Life
Is like a game
Life
Is not to be wasted
Life
Long of fun, short of love
Life
Has touched my heart.

Bradley Giles (11)
Hextable School, Swanley

Home Sweet Home - Haiku

Mother, father, safe
TV, games, family, sweet
Home sweet home, with love.

Matthew Abery (13)
Hextable School, Swanley

Wake Up! Wake Up!

Wake up! Wake up! See what you're doing!
Can't you see you're bringing the Earth to ruin?
All the things you take for granted are slowly disappearing
The trees that grow and the birds that soar above
You will no longer be hearing.

Does it please you to choke the Earth by the throat?
Determined are you to destroy our protective coat
Our seas' and rivers' parts no longer blue
But as black as raven's wings as the oil slicks spew.

Do you enjoy it? Causing the animals to die?
Because when I think of that, I just start to cry
The trees are falling down, one by one
What are you going to do next? Darken down the sun?

So wake up! Wake up! And see what you're doing
Can't you see you're bringing the Earth to ruin?
All the things that you take for granted are slowly disappearing
So change your heart, mind and ways
And we can carry on living our days.

Chloe Andrews (12)
Hextable School, Swanley

Peter Osgood

Born is the King of Stamford Bridge
100 odd games, 100 odd goals
Not man but machine.

Osgood, Osgood

Born is the King of Stamford Bridge
Legend, legend, world class
The best there ever was
King of the Bridge

Osgood!

Drew Smith (12)
Hextable School, Swanley

Bullying!

There I was on my own
I had a big bad groan
Being kicked about all day
I am trying to say hey
They're not stopping so I cry
When it comes to it, I lie.

All my friends run away when they see a bully
I try not to look woolly
Let the world all be nice
Try not to get head lice
I am going to have to tell
So why don't all the victims yell?

I am beating bullying today
Have to do something, yay
They are getting told off
I nearly had a cough
So they have been beaten and defeated
Now I am happy as a clown as they make me feel big again.

Bradley Niven (12)
Hextable School, Swanley

Frank Lampard

When he scores a goal he's always looking up in the sky
To remember his mum who's up high in the sky.

The children always look up to him
When he scores that final goal
And the crowd's roaring!
Roaring! Like a lion.

Lampard and Terry always on the ball
Terry is defending then Terry gets the ball
Crosses it to Lampard who controls the ball
He shoots and scores!

Bryce Turner (13)
Hextable School, Swanley

Abuse

I erupt inside with pain
Astonished of the fearsome cane
Another day has gone in depression
Because my father unleashes fury and aggression
He must get a lot of joy
Throwing me around like a toy.

My dad shows signs of weakening
Because people are peeking in
I think my father is showing some care
Because he's losing his evil glare
Now he's started making dinner
He's slowing, proving he's a winner.

Now we've started going out
I'm slowly beginning to lose my doubt
'Son, I have a mighty treasure
That I give to you in great pleasure
Now I can hold you close to my heart
So here's a beginning of a brand new start!'

Joshua Darren Newman (12)
Hextable School, Swanley

Jade Goody

If she was still here there would be no tears
No fears, just jolly Jade and her wicked ways

Everyone will miss her because she was a good mum to the two boys
Good friend and good person to know

We feel for Jade's boys, Bobby and Freddie
Because they will never see their mummy again
But in out hearts she will always be known
As Golden Goody forever!

We can be like her too, just think of your family.

Sharona Kennard (12)
Hextable School, Swanley

Anti-Bullying

One day I went to play
To have a little joke
But then a big boy
Came and gave me a poke.

He was very tall
And scary he was
He liked a lot of fun
But then he fell on his bum.

He was a big bully
And liked to hit and smack
He also had a big rucksack.

I showed him the way
Of things to be seen
He then became as
Polite as the Queen
We soon became friends
Like you've never seen.

Chloe Guichard (12)
Hextable School, Swanley

Enjoy Your Life

Life is short, life is unfair
Enjoy it while it lasts
Have some fun, lots of fun
Hopefully it has just begun.
Don't moan, don't groan
Enjoy being a kid.
Life is short, so come on let's
Have a lot of fun!
Play football, ride a bike
Think or do whatever you like, party all night!
Let's enjoy life; you're only a kid once!

Jordan Chambers (12)
Hextable School, Swanley

Bullying

A child crying after school
Why? Because of a bully calling her names all day
He was calling her names like 'Mad Mary'
And it didn't end there.

He grabbed her favourite toy and he dropped
It down the gutter
He then laughed like a hyena and walked off
She went home crying that night too scared to tell anyone.

But then one day she stood up and told someone
And eventually it was stopped
Unfortunately there are some children who are being
Threatened with the iron fist
So I hope that one day everyone will get along
And there will be an end to bullying.

Kieran Manning (11)
Hextable School, Swanley

Why Pick On Me?

As I walked down the street
They came as one big fleet
Shouting and screaming at me, perhaps if they didn't
I'd be smiling with glee
Fear going through my veins
Which causes many pains
I wish that I could make them stop
Then I'd have to explain from the top.

Words can't describe how much I hate this
My old peaceful life I miss
The pushing, the shoving
I wish they could be loving
Or at least have a small bit of care
A good life we could then share.

Olivia Fox-Porritt (12)
Hextable School, Swanley

Stop Bullying

I have had enough with bullying
Bullying makes me sick
It's like a child has nothing to pick
Most people think it's worrying
Others say it's horrific
But the bullies say it's terrific.

The thing I hate most about bullying
Is when they bully disabled people
They are defenceless. They can't do anything
But experience it.

I want to put an end to this
But it's such a hard thing to do
Well, we need your help too.

Robert Johnson (12)
Hextable School, Swanley

War

I walked out of my house
And saw a terrible sight
A valley of bodies
There, lying through the night
I could only see them by the moonlight.

I knew some of their faces, they lived near me
A lot of them young faces, that's all I could see
Walking over a pool of blood
All the soldiers covered in mud.

This should not be the sight we see
These young boys do not get the chance to be
The bodies will be burned by the local church
The families of the soldiers, permanently hurt.

Samuel Anderson-Eade (13)
Hextable School, Swanley

Jade Goody

She's done so well 'cause she
Went through hell
With her children, cancer and life
She's got 2 beautiful boys
She survived the press
But she is put to rest
Better than being in her awful mess
Jade Goody did so well
She was as brave as a lion through her mess
But now she is put to rest.

RIP

Jade Goody.

Rebecca O'Shea (12)
Hextable School, Swanley

Jade Goody

Jade Goody was full of joy,
she liked buying her kids toys.

She sent a message to all the
girls, to look out for yourselves
and take care of your health.

She lived her life in front of the camera
she acted herself 'cause it didn't matter.

When the angels came on the
day they did, it could be no
other day than Mother's Day.

RIP Jade Goody!

Ellie Teather (13)
Hextable School, Swanley

Bullying Is Not Right

B ullying is not right
U nderstand the bullying might
L ike a shadow in the night
L ittle Tommy is filled with fright
Y elling and screaming in his ear
I s the bully somewhere near?
N ot a very happy sight.
G laring, grasping everyone is gasping
That spot was like a two-man stage
Tommy against a monster's rage
Go get a teacher, there's going to be a fight
Quick before one loses his light.

Ross Eyles (11)
Hextable School, Swanley

Murder

Murder is a word for madness
No one deserves to be killed
Why would someone take a life?
How could someone take a life?
A mystery which shall never be found
A human shot down to the ground
It is so unnecessary
It is so sad
People who murder
Are truly mad.

Andrew Leitch (13)
Hextable School, Swanley

Fire

They start off as small as ants
They get as big as a man
Eventually they're the size of a house
With smoke as tall as a skyscraper
The fire burns like the sun on a hot day
The deadly smoke hunts out the people in quick, swift movements
Within a few minutes the cries have stopped
The fire eventually stops
There is silence.

Sean Baines
Hextable School, Swanley

My Passion - Haiku

Deep blue water shines
In the bright morning sunshine
What a lovely day.

Danny Booth
Hextable School, Swanley

I Have A Dream - Haiku

Moto GP, best
Valentino Rossi, fast
Speeding around track.

Ben Fuller (13)
Hextable School, Swanley

If You Have A Dream

If you have a dream
Stick by it forever
Start straight from the beginning
No's not an answer, never.

Actress or singer
Teacher or dentist
Lawyer or doctor
Nurse or apprentice.

If you have a dream
Simply let yourself go
Run for it, reach
And never say no.

Keep yourself on top
Never let yourself down
Keep up a warm smile
Don't let them see you frown.

You're always a winner
Losing isn't the answer
Think positive and you'll win
Optician, even dancer.

I have a dream
I'll stick by it forever
I'm gonna start from the beginning
And I won't give up, ever.

Samantha Cox (11)
Honywood Community Science School, Coggeshall

Lost In A Book

Your head is lost in a book
Your mind has drifted away
You're in a different world
And there you want to stay.

Oblivious of things around you
Your eyes resting on word after word
Your mind is in the story line
No sounds surrounding you heard.

Imagination running free
All the characters become real
Wondering what will be on the next page
Gripped and excited you feel.

You're on the final chapter
All the mysteries will unfold
You're disappointed that it's near the end
And you'll come out of your special world.

Because of this, I have a dream
That in years to come, one day
I'll become a children's book writer
And write stories, poems or a play.

I hope that if my dream comes true
My work will be enjoyed
By *all* children, near or far
Whether a girl or a boy.

Then . . .

Their heads will be lost in *my* book
Their minds will have drifted away
They'll be in a different world
And there they'll want to stay.

Eleanor Page (11)
Honywood Community Science School, Coggeshall

Dreams Of Kids

Every kid's dream is to become a pop star
To reach the top and go further than far
To move their family to Hollywood or LA
In a sensational house and be able to pay.

To not have to go to a proper school
To look out to the garden and see a massive pool
To wake up every morning and arrive at a set
See other famous people I've already met.

To walk down red carpets and see screaming fans
To travel the world to visit distant lands
Out at concerts and always on tour
Your schedule is always full and that's for sure.

Being a star can be lots of fun
Especially when you're still quite young
But there is a chance that you just might
Ruin it for yourself and turn off the light.

Yes may I say if you are not careful
And your family do not stay incredibly prayerful
You might just find yourself at a sticky end
With nowhere to go, no sign of a bend.

Anyway, let's move on to a more positive end
With parties and gifts and time with your friends
I will now leave you on this sunny day
But before, a few things I would like to say.

If there is a chance to reach your dream
Then go for it girl and watch everyone beam
Before I leave you there is just one thing to say
If you are working for something you really want

Never give up!

Annabelle Randall (11)
Honywood Community Science School, Coggeshall

Life Is What You Make It

When I was young I watched my mum
Having so much fun on board
The bell would go
And off she went
Faster and faster Frosty would go.

Round they went over the fences
Mum was a-kicking
Frosty's tail was a-swishing
A roar from the crowd
A clear round was achieved
Hooray, hooray, my mum is great!

Now I have a goal
That I must beat
Clip clop on the dot
Trying to achieve my best shot.

Hearing people cheer for me
Helps me to become what I like to be
Trying to achieve to be a famous horse rider
That would be the best for me.

Trying to be like Ellen Whitaker or Lucinda Green
Or even to perform at Olympia
That would be the best thing for me
Getting the best horse
Would be a dream!

I like being a dreamer
I can then achieve all my goals
I hope in the real world it will all become true
Life is the real world!

Lucinda May (12)
Honywood Community Science School, Coggeshall

Dream

Do you have a dream?
Do you shout? Do you scream?
Your dream can come true
Just think it through.

You decide whether your dream comes true
I can make my dream come true too
Dreams are meant to be difficult
That's why they're dreams.

You may not know what you want to be
Just think, write a poem, like me
Write about a thing you like
For example riding a bike.

I know what I want to be
I want to teach people PE
Just like I got taught
Running round and playing sports.

Dreams are like aspirations
If you know what you aspire to do
You know what you want to do
If you fail, try again and again and again.

So try to make your dream come true
Don't worry if you don't know what to do
All the best careers
Are made up on the way.

Lauren Mudle (11)
Honywood Community Science School, Coggeshall

It's A Dreamers World

I have a goal, a vision to be
In the Olympics and become a hero.

To hear the crowd cheering for me
Would be immense and what an achievement that would be
To feel my heart pounding and my trembling feet
Waiting by the starting line and to see a million pairs of eyes
All staring at me!

The atmosphere around me, I feel so alive
Then a whisper telling me to stand by
I get into position, my ears on red alert
A gust of wind widens my head
Just thinking about all those dreamers lying in bed.

'Go' and I'm off, desperate for that 1st place
My legs and feet pushing me to the limit, I'm on fire!
I'm still shaking with fear and excitement but as strong as
A sword I did it
I crossed the line seconds ahead
I won and with that, my heart and I were very content.

So dreamers out there, don't give up just yet
Stay strong and fight for your goal
And some day you might just get there.

Zoe Goate (12)
Honywood Community Science School, Coggeshall

Friends And Enemies

I believe that we shouldn't have enemies
For 'Hate' is a very strong word
I believe that we shouldn't have enemies
Because deep down, you're really good friends.

I believe that we shouldn't have enemies
It doesn't get you very far
I believe that we shouldn't have enemies
Being mean isn't that nice.

I believe that we shouldn't have enemies
It's all just because of jealousy
I believe that we shouldn't have enemies
And be friends instead.

Because . . .

A friend is someone that you can trust
Who is there for you during your ups and downs
A friend is someone who believes in you
And would never want you to change.

Enemies will never be, but
Friendship is like a ring
It will never, ever end.

Eloise Webster (12)
Honywood Community Science School, Coggeshall

What Should I Do?

I had a thought on what to be
I thought, *I want to teach.*
Maybe English
Language
Art
Or science.
Maths
Music or
Technology.
Drama
Business
Or teach PE.

I like cricket
Running
Basketball.
Rugby
Football
Tennis.
I love to swim and
Gymnastics.

What do you think I should do?

Brett Franklin-Maddock (11)
Honywood Community Science School, Coggeshall

My Dream Job

Lying in my bed at night
I think of when I am older
In my mind I have got a dream
And that is to be a book writer.

All the fun you must have
Writing all those books
Adventure, fairy tale and fantasy
They will be my genres.

Maybe I could illustrate too
Drawing colourful pictures
Putting them in my books
It will be brilliant!

My books will sell out rapidly
And will be in the shop windows
Children asking their mum and dad
'They look good, can I get one please?'

But the only way to achieve your dream
Is to work very hard
But there is another way
And that is to never give up!

Emily Vincent (12)
Honywood Community Science School, Coggeshall

I Have An Ambition

I have an ambition
To be a musician
To be able to play to millions of people
Sharing my music with them

I have an ambition
To be a musician
Touring the world in a private jet
Signing autographs for all my fans

I have an ambition
To be a musician
To stand on stage, crowd applauding
The music pulsating through my veins

I have an ambition
To be a musician
Expressing my feelings in the songs I write
Hoping to sell them for lots of cash

I have an ambition
To be a musician
The feel of the strings and clutching the pick
The rock music rings through my veins.

Alec Scott (12)
Honywood Community Science School, Coggeshall

The Soldiers

Soldiers are inspiring
For us they are firing
But every day they are dying
Just for our protection.

Without them we'd be overrun
They are really number one
But every day they are dying
Just for our protection.

You can't call them lame
Because for them it's no game
But every day they are dying
Just for our protection.

Not often do they go home
To see the good old garden gnome
But every day they are dying
Just for our protection.

So let's all remember them
We might get a big gem
But every day they are dying
Just for our protection.

Andrew Swinnerton (12)
Honywood Community Science School, Coggeshall

When I Grow Up

When I grow up
I would like to teach, and take my family down to the beach.
I'll have two children, Maisie and Dylan,
And I'll fill their sandwiches with sandwich filling.
When I grow up,
My husband will be loving, caring to our kids and me.
We'll have got married on a summer's day
And to our honeymoon suite we ran away!
When I grow up
I will teach class 4, all of the children will come rushing through the door
We'll go on school trips and have loads of fun,
And they will enjoy school until the day is done.
When I grow up
I will feed my dog and every morning I'll
Go out for a jog!
I will look after the children who cry
and help every one of them who are shy.
When I grow up
I would like to teach, and take my family down to the beach
My kids will be called Dyllan and Maisie
and they will both be really crazy!

Eleanor Hutchinson (12)
Honywood Community Science School, Coggeshall

I Have A Dream

I have a dream that everybody could live in peace without war
Everyone could live together
I have a dream that the men in the armed forces could
Come back from the wars untouched because people
Had stopped fighting.

I have a dream that bullies who were hitting their
Victims would realise that it is wrong to hurt
That they should say sorry and forget about it.

I have a dream that racism would be forgotten and
Should never be used
Treat others how you would like to be treated.

I have a dream that all the countries and all the people
In the world would be nice to each other, care for each
Other and get on well.

I have a dream that our world could be a place to enjoy
And to have fun
Peace not war
Good not bad and
Loving not hateful.

Mark Cordeiro (12)
Honywood Community Science School, Coggeshall

I Have A Dream

I have a dream that people would stop hating each other
I have a dream that world hunger would end
I have a dream that there is world peace
I have a dream that money wouldn't take over the world
I have a dream that pollution would end
I have a dream that sickness would stop
I have a dream the people would be equal
I have a dream that people would respect me for who I am
I have a dream that everybody would have this dream.

Danielle Thompson (12)
Honywood Community Science School, Coggeshall

My Dream

I have been to many places
Many regions of the world
Everyone silent as I am shown
Being lifted by one of the most famous
Sports people in the world.
So beautiful, big and bright
Seeing everything as I go.

Everyone's there to make their country proud
The adrenalin rush as they walk out
Waiting for their chance to make themselves known
For their chance to be in the spotlight
Practising all their life for this day
I see it all.

Seeing things behind the scenes
Everyone getting ready for their big event
And after the event has finished
I get placed around the winner's neck
Seeing their country scream for them
Is the best thing I will ever hear.

Holly Street (12)
Honywood Community Science School, Coggeshall

Operation Black Storm

This is it, the final push
To stamp out terror in Afghanistan
You walk through the desert
No matter what the conditions
Thank you for all you've done.

This is it, the final push
You think of your friends and family at home
You think about your bed
And how you were there
Thank you for all you've done.

This is it, the final push
You stand strong and firm to serve your country
Your squad become brothers
This is Operation Black Storm
Thank you for all you've done.

Matthew Ward (12)
Honywood Community Science School, Coggeshall

I Am Dreaming!

Starving people sitting dying
Whilst we sit gorging ourselves,
Tummies rumbling, can't hardly move.
Energy drinks, doing Olympics,
Tongues gone dry
Water too far away
Not enough energy to walk.
Babies crying, wanting food.
I'm dreaming of a better life
Where everyone is happy.
Smiling, laughing, with all joyfulness,
I'm dreaming of a better world
Where everyone has food.

Rebecca Miller (12)
Honywood Community Science School, Coggeshall

I Have A Dream . . .

I have a dream to be one of those vets
All those animals suffering no more
Curing each and every one of those ill pets
Wild wolves can howl, untamed tigers can roar
The fish can swim without the slightest fear
Exotic animals can stay at home
Not allowed to kill a single poor deer
Black and white stallions can stay in Rome
Put a stop to all the horrific zoos
Beating any animal is a crime
All horrible circuses, ha, you lose
Please look at my hopes and dreams in a rhyme
I have a dream to be one of those vets
Curing each and every one of those ill pets.

Ryan Collins (11)
Honywood Community Science School, Coggeshall

Let's Dance

I have a dream
Not to be in a football team
But to become an elegant, graceful ballet dancer
And answer the questions I have to answer.

Ballerinas look perfectly stunning
And stick to skipping, definitely not running.
As I twirl on my pointed toes
Making sure the dance flows.

As I glissade to the right
I prance into the air like a kite
And gorgeously give a gleaming smile
Which would beam for a mile.

Charlotte Wilkins (12)
Honywood Community Science School, Coggeshall

The Young Broken Heart

There's a wound that will never heal because of you
Through the pain and hurt that you caused
Like a scar that will never heal.

You could have heard my voice if I had told
But my voice was too low
As you were in your play world
While I was struck in the middle of this hurt
And you still can't hear my voice.

Start listening to me
I'm not a rag doll
I'm a child
Open your ears and your heart
Coz my heart's broken and needs love
So everyone listen to my message
Coz I'm bringing it to you
Make sure the child that is hurt is heard
Coz life is not all it's cracked up to be
But if you hear me it might change!

Emma Johnson (16)
Integrated Support Service, Harlow

Life And Death

Life, it's a wonderful thing,
But death is right round the corner,
It strikes you in the back like nobody knows.
Once there's life, you know there's death.

The chance to live is fantastic,
You get the happiness, the joy, the hope.
People in your life look out for you, they're called friends.
But other people sometimes wonder, *why is there death?*
And other people don't understand that life comes with
consequences, *this is death.*

Kieran O'Donoghue (12)
Kingsbrook School, Milton Keynes

I Have A Dream!

I have a dream!
Where racism was just a myth,
Where people got past religion, race and colour.

I have a dream!
Where people no longer have to hide
In fear of what others may think.

I have a dream!
Where poverty, pain and inequality
Is just a scary story wise ones told.

I have a dream!
Where thoughts, dreams and hopes
Were respected, not dismissed at first glance.

I have a dream!
Where war is a folk tale
Not a fact.

I have a dream!
The feelings of love, passion and forgiveness
Replaced hate, indifference and revenge.

I have a dream!
Where people saw you for your personality
No what you have or look like.

I have a dream!
Where countries helped each other,
Rather than watch them suffer.

I have a dream!
Where the planet wasn't dying
By the selfish hands of mankind!

Yes, this is my dream!
If we worked together
This dream could be a reality . . .

Jess Jenkins (14)
Kingsbrook School, Milton Keynes

The True Meaning Of Amity

I've been walking through your streets
Where diminutive money is earned.
Where all your buildings are crying
And oblivious neckties working.

Overbearing advertising.
God of exploitation.
Mirrorism, filtering information for the public eye.
Designed for profiteering.

Condemnations
Coupled with globalisation.

Unnecessary death.

Manufacturing consent is the name of the game.
Money - the bottom line.

Four thousand hungry children leave us per hour from starvation,
While billions are spent on bombs!
Creating death showers!
Nobody is concerned!

Excluding me. You. Us.
I have a dream that all nations will rise up
And live the true meaning of amity.

I have a dream that the prey will
Sit at the table of harmony with the predators.

I have a dream all past, future and present conflict will die
And the mountains of unity will rise.

Yes; you, me, them, they - equals.
We all can find exquisite delight
In the abundance of peace.

Yes, I have a dream.

Katie Maddams (13)
Kingsbrook School, Milton Keynes

Why Me?

I'm only eight years old,
So small, delicate and scared.
I always get the blame
When I haven't done anything wrong.

I'm black and blue all over,
Broken bones and everything.
It's my parents,
They have a frozen, black heart.

My parents have everything,
I have nothing.
Just because we're a little poor,
They say it's my fault.

When I ask for a little something,
I'm whipped, I'm punched, do I need to say more?
While they relax, having a good time,
I do the housework, cooking, or sleeping on the floor.

My mum, dad, gran and grandpa,
All hate me, I'm unloved.
I get no sleep as I cry for freedom,
Lying in a cold, dark room like all their hearts.

Why me? Why?
I'll do anything.
I'd rather live on the streets
Than be at home.

I'm only eight years old,
So small, delicate and scared.
I always get the blame
When I haven't done anything wrong.

Emilie Dear (13)
Kingsbrook School, Milton Keynes

I Can Only Imagine

I can only imagine
The world whitewashed in peace
Pure and clean, not dirty
Burning bright, not gloomy.

No wars, no anger, no fighting
No lack, no want, no wishing
We'll all have what we want to have
We'll all be who we want to be.

I can only imagine
The day I'm truly happy
I'll look in the mirror and like what I see
Stand up, speak out, no fear of being me.

I can only imagine
When our great big world
Is a vibrant technicolour dream?

I'll wear a lime green coat with a yellow skirt
A red waistcoat with an orange shirt
I'll light up the world with my rainbow of colour
Sing on the rooftops and watch people follow.

I can only imagine
I simply just dream
Of no lies, no hurt, no wicked schemes.

Will the things that I speak of manifest as true?
Will we stand here, unlabelled, just me and just you?
Will we fly? Will we float on the dove's wings of peace?
The handcuffs of burden unlocked with relief . . .

I can only imagine.

Blessing Shammah (15)
Kingsbrook School, Milton Keynes

Life With Lies

There's always one who thinks they're alone,
Cold and dark with nowhere to turn,
The dark abyss closing around you,
Full of pain and lies,
Lies for why they do it to you,
Lies for when they're going to stop,
But there is no end,
No help, only the driving will of them to stop,
That you can only give to yourself,
They only do it because you are small,
And unworthy, but really you are the most powerful of all,
So shout for them to stop,
To stop your suffering and pain,
But they will not listen to all that happens,
So wait till the dawn when the sun rises high,
And that day will come when the sun rises,
And then people might realise what happens
To those who get beaten,
Again and again and again,
But not because their parents have no pity or life,
They do it because they're angry or sad,
Or to drain the life and hope of those who
Fight for life and a family who loves them,
And the dreams of those who love them fall away,
The dreams don't stop coming even after it is over,
They come in the day and they come at night,
But only to those who don't fight,
For rights of life and a life with no pain,
But that day only comes when the sun rises.

Emily Hill (13)
Kingsbrook School, Milton Keynes

Where Do I Belong?

Why take a chance?
You see the people you want to be.
You're surrounded by a world you don't believe in.

Why take a chance?
The straights and curls on every strand of hair
Confuse you deep within.

Why take a chance?
You're worried to step into your reflection
And what you might see.

Why take a chance?
You stand on your own in a corner,
Glancing over to see
The pretty, perky, popular girls gossiping and laughing.

Why take a chance?
You've tried it once you'll try it again,
But you know within your soul,
The wadded brick that lay on your desk,
You're dying to go and read.

Why take a chance?
Your mum went out the other day
To get you some things you wanted,
She brought them up in a plastic bag,
Placed it on your bed.
You sit silently,
Thinking and wondering why?

Why take a chance?

Cara Salmon (13)
Kingsbrook School, Milton Keynes

What's Wrong With That?

A girl is driving in her sports car
Wearing her lucky football shirt
The car is nice and shiny,
The top is caked in dirt
Her football boots are old and worn,
Her hair is like she woke at dawn.

What's wrong with that?

The boy runs through his book of music
Wearing a big hat
And a cardigan saying 'Love songs'.

What's wrong with that?

Her friends they laugh, 'Go have a bath'
They mutter in her ear
'So what' she says 'I love football,
It's all I have to do since school,
I love this game like a bar of chocolate
So I don't care 'cause it is my talent.'

What's wrong with that?

He grows his hair and shows his friends
They say, 'Get a life
Take off that cardigan, it's blooming pink
Just grab some skates and come to the ice rink.'
He says, 'No, my love for dance is honestly true,
It's my passion, you just don't have a clue.'

What's wrong with that?

Nicole Knott (12)
Kingsbrook School, Milton Keynes

The Lady Who Changed Everything

Men dying,
Hope fading,
Life ending,
Men crying,
Nothing to make them live.

Men waiting,
Men hoping,
Lady with the lamp walking,
As she passes they kiss her shadow.

Men eating,
Men sleeping,
Men reading,
Things improving,
They are getting better, all because of the lady.

Lady writing,
Lady arguing,
Lady working,
Men living,
The world is changing.

Lady winning,
Lady is changing,
But for how long?

Lady is dying,
But still lives.

Harriet Chinn (12)
Kingsbrook School, Milton Keynes

Grampy

I just want to make it clear
My love for you will never disappear,
I love you more each and every day
And remember you in my own special way.

We wish you didn't have to go
For everyone loves you so.
You were my grampy and my friend
And I wonder if my heart will ever mend.

Our lives won't ever be the same
But we know that you're not to blame,
As God wanted you up there with Him
To help make all His angels sing.

Their loving verse that I won't hear
Until the day when I am near
You again right by my side
My time I will always bide.

I love you Grampy and always will
And it seems like time has stood still,
But to be with you again one day
Remember me I will always pray.

All there is left to say
Is I love you Grampy
I'll see you again one day
All my love now and forever.

Nicolle Mattinson (15)
Kingsbrook School, Milton Keynes

We Are Blind

How can we not see it?
How can we ignore it?
It's the state of mind to judge someone.
It's the state of mind to make fun.
How can we start to tackle the problem?
Just put your hand up and admit to it.
Why do we see the image first?
Is it a curse?

Did the Devil place judgement on us?
Can't we see people for who they are?
We are blind, we are unkind.
Do we have to wind back the clock to see happy faces?

In years we will age and will come to a stage when looks do not matter.
The heart is as precious as gold.
We all believe what we are told.
We're not rubbish,
We're people
With lives to live
And people to be with . . .

'Mirror mirror on the wall, who's the fairest of them all?'
A cover girl, a beauty queen
Is that all?

Should we remind ourselves to ask
What is really behind the mask?

Lauren Smyth (14)
Kingsbrook School, Milton Keynes

Grandad Billy

Sitting there smoking away,
That's the problem with kids today,
I told you once, I told you twice,
Don't by silly,
Do you want to end up like your grandad Billy,
Lying there in a little brown box.
Remember the day we changed his socks,
The tumour was the one to blame,
This is the thing that put his life to shame.
Sitting there eating his brain away,
When the dreaded day finally came,
Grandad Billy knew smoking and drinking ain't no game.
I didn't know what to say
When the priest was standing there chatting away,
I felt like falling to my knees and fading away
With the look of sadness,
On my mother's face,
The look of disappointment and disgrace.
At that moment a tear came to my eye,
I fell to the floor and began to cry.
Now I know the sadness and pain,
My life will never be the same again.
My thoughts on drugs have changed,
Now I know,
Smoking and drinking ain't no game.

Daniel Clarke (15)
Kingsbrook School, Milton Keynes

Bless Her

Bless her, my poor grandma,
Who cannot walk very far,
She has struggled all her life
But is a great mum, nan and wife!

Bless her

She can hardly walk up the stairs,
She seems to think that no one cares,
Although we help her every day,
She has to do it her own way.

Bless her

I think of her all the time,
But it brings a tear to my eyes,
At night i dreamt that she was well,
To live a life free from Hell
But when I woke, it fell apart,
When she's in pain it breaks my heart.

Bless her

My nanny is so special to me,
I wish she could live pain-free.
I love her so,
She's my hero.

Bless her.

Holly-Anastasia Becks (13)
Kingsbrook School, Milton Keynes

Heroes Of The Olympics!

Think of the heroes of the Olympics,
All of them full of talent.
Each one of them successful,
Because they are so gallant.

Running, swimming, cycling
Kelly, Rebecca, the real McHoy.

Think of the heroes of the Olympics,
All heroes we want to see.
They made our country proud,
Especially you and me.

Running, swimming, cycling
Kelly, Rebecca, the real McHoy.

Think of the heroes of the Olympics,
Training hard every day.
Could that be you?
Somehow, some way.

Running, swimming, cycling
Kelly, Rebecca, the real McHoy.

Think of the heroes of the Olympics,
Pure gold, glittering medals, given to them around their neck.
Standing up there,
An emotional moment, they'll never forget.

Rebecca Folwell (12)
Kingsbrook School, Milton Keynes

A Shoulder To Lean On

I have a dream,
A dream that made the world a better place.
Where no one was rich
And no one was poor,
And when we would falter
We would always have a shoulder to lean on.

Where people had shelter
And not the cold stubborn air,
And instead of nothing, they had clothes to wear,
And when we would falter
We would always have a shoulder to lean on.

People came together as one community,
No conflict, no fights, no war,
Freedom,
And when we would falter
We would always have a shoulder to lean on.

The dream I had
Made the world evolve,
Made people come together
And changed us all.
Now we all know
That if we ever would falter
We always have a shoulder to lean on.

Gemma Hall (14)
Kingsbrook School, Milton Keynes

Why? Just Ask Yourself Why?

Lots of people live in houses
But think
What about those homeless people?
Those kids with rich parents
Just keep wanting more and more
But why?
Ask yourself why
Isn't what they've got enough?
At parties they have snacks for food
But then that becomes old news
They chuck it away
And that's just a waste
As those homeless people are starving
The popular kids walk around
Like they're the best
They give no donations to any nation
But why?
Ask yourself why
Do a good thing for poor people
Because no one cares about them
They are suffering, dying
And probably, most definitely, crying
But why?
Ask yourself why.

Amanda Walton (12)
Kingsbrook School, Milton Keynes

Beauty

Should we be more like the wind,
A rainbow, dew or mist?
For it's beauty is there,
But is it real,
Or is beauty as thin as the air?

Should we be judged by our outer shell,
Or is it what's inside?
Do not judge yourself by what's in the mirror,
As your mirror could certainly lie.

Should we have a second chance,
A second first impression?
We shouldn't be grouped
By our lipgloss, mascara and blusher.

It's the person inside that really counts,
Our true inner beauty,
We shouldn't care
About background, colour and hair.

Should we be more like the wind,
A rainbow, dew or mist?
For its beauty is there,
But is it real,
Or is beauty as thin as the air?

Ellie Coppins (11)
Kingsbrook School, Milton Keynes

I Have A Dream . . .

I have a dream that there is no war, no violence, just equality.
I have a dream that there is no weapons and no reason to
kill each other.
I have a dream that global warming doesn't exist and nothing
is living in fear of when the world will end.
I have a dream that no racism or bullying occurs and it was just 'fashion'
back in the day.
I have a dream that there will be no diseases and no sudden
endings to life.
I have a dream that there will be a cure for cancer, no long
term suffering.
I have a dream that the seven deadly sins were only just a myth.
I have a dream that poverty was just a lie to get money.
I have a dream that money wasn't the key to all evil.
I have a dream that gun shops were replaced with sweet shops.
I have a dream that groups with guns turned to helping the OAPs.
I have a dream that the wars between the Taliban and the US would stop
the violence.
I have a dream that everyone was judged the same.
I had this dream,
It was a very good dream
But I know it will never be reality.
Will it?

Emily Quinn (15)
Kingsbrook School, Milton Keynes

Was It Worth It

Bang, bang, a fatal moment
Bang, bang, a family broken
The hooded stranger ran away
Leaving the victim alone and strayed.

The silent killer in his bed.
All the thoughts running through his head
Why did he do it was it worth it?
Why? why did he do it?

The killer stayed in his room
Time bleeding like the wound he created
Knock, knock, at the door, the police stormed
His life was over.

He was taken away by the law enforcing police
His life was in cuffs
Trapped in a cell like his childhood in his head
Why did he do it? What was the point?

Trapped in a cell for years and years
The killer whipped out the policeman's gun
Bang, bang, the killer was dead
Bang, bang, the killer was put to bed.

Jordan Easterbrook (13)
Kingsbrook School, Milton Keynes

Dream Paths

No matter how hard you try,
You feel you'll have the same old life
Whether you're twenty or seventy,
You can always achieve your destiny.

If you put your mind to it,
Anything is possible
If you don't go for it,
You will be a fool.

When you reach your dream
It will come to you,
Life may be mean
But cows will always go moo . . .

Focus on your future,
And not on the past
Dream and dream,
And it will last.
Pixies and fairies don't exist
So get your head out of the clouds
And focus on this.

Shauni Read (13)
Kingsbrook School, Milton Keynes

I Saw It

I saw it. Hope, despair.
I saw the old woman
cry tears by a rainy window when her war hero husband
didn't come home.
I saw the bullet
raging and sweating fear as it pierced the heart of a kid bystander.
I saw the mother's grieving face as a wasted life slept in a small coffin -
swallowed by the ground.
I saw the generations of ethnic race -
ankles in chains and families dead.
We hold the guilt for those dead.
We hold the guilt. The pain.
But now I see the old woman
happy in her age. A frail hand reads hope and a future that will be.
The bullet has faded now. Just a ghost. A scar.
There are no bullets, no guns.
Black and white are all as one.
Parts of a person that make a whole.
Now I see it. Hope. But not despair.
Despair has gone. It is lost.

Cecilia Wray (14)
Kingsbrook School, Milton Keynes

One Day!

Who truly know the beauty of true love?
Love and kindness can touch our lives once
And last for a full lifetime.
One day I'll wake and love will have engulfed our precious world.
Sadness and suffering will be banished and only joy will remain
But how long will that be? We can only hope.
Love fills so many books and yet it cannot fill our tiny planet.
Forever love will warm people's patient hearts.
But with such a wonderful thing in the world
Why must crime, disease and poverty strike?
One day we'll get all the homeless people off the streets
And welcome back all those who have been missing.
All you have to do is believe and hope with all your heart.
It may be on your left side but it's always right.
We should all be more interested in the future.
After all, that is where we are going to spend the rest of our lives
We should care more about our future dreams than our past.
One day we shall forget all the problems of our planet.
Live as a big family. That is my dream and one day I hope it's a reality.
That one day could be today!

Sapphire Lewis (14)
Kingsbrook School, Milton Keynes

World Dream

Should the world be full of destruction and pain?
Nobody should have to fight in the world of today.
We can always have a say,
We don't have to act like animals,
War should not walk our lands,
We should join our hands,
Unite the world.

No litter on our sands,
We should recycle our cans,
Save the trees,
Polar bears should be free,
We all hold the key to world peace,
We can unlock it, you and me.

This is a world with no inequality,
Everyone should mix,
Everyone has their qualities.
This is my dream,
A dream I share,
This is the dream of a perfect world.

Daniel Streeter (14)
Kingsbrook School, Milton Keynes

Tomorrow

I had a dream that all conflict
had vanished from our kind.
I had a dream that all wars were
just faded memories in our minds . . .
Reminders of how young and foolish
the human race once was.

I had a dream that all racism,
sexism and faith quarrels
were absurd and alien to us,
overshadowed by mutual morals.
I had a dream that we were happy,
smiling, with eyes open to justice.
That our laughter was caused
by the joy of others
and not by apparent suffrage.

I didn't have a dream last night,
I had a prophesy
of a future more than possible,
in our grasp, easily.

Giselle Sadler (15)
Kingsbrook School, Milton Keynes

Stop Poverty

People are dying
Suffering, crying
Poverty, hunger
The silent killer!

The torture, the pain
The grieving, the strain
Eating them inside out
It makes them scream and shout

Even in Britain, England right now
People suffer from poverty somehow
20,000 die each day
Some say we can't stop it no way!

All the food we do not need
That we buy out of pure greed
People need or they may die
We can all make a difference, go on just try

Do something special, donate some food
It could save one life or even a brood.

Rosie Johnson (12)
Kingsbrook School, Milton Keynes

My Special Person Poem

This is a person I have known for many years since I was born.
He has been there through the good times and the bad times.
When I'm sad he is always there for me.
When I got hit he was also there for me.
I cheer him on to get a try for his rugby team.
I help him do the things he can't.
If he wasn't there I couldn't look up to him
I couldn't cheer him on for his team.
He is only 14, he is in Year 9,
If someone talks badly about him I won't listen.

Harry Mears (12)
Kingsbrook School, Milton Keynes

A World Without War

I had a dream of war,
but beautiful,
no blood, no guts, no gore.
Just peace and harmony,
flowers and hearts.
Why this heartless suffering?
Just think for a moment,
of a world with no war.
But is it meant to be like that?
Would it be weird without war?
Like a school without teachers,
or an elephant without a trunk.
It would be very strange.
I hope to share this dream
but secretly I know it will
Never,
never,
ever
come true.

Adam Pooley (14)
Kingsbrook School, Milton Keynes

Daydream

I see it all. Hope, despair.
Sunshine and rain. Dreams and nightmares.
Imagine the world free of war,
Free of poverty, greed and gore.
No anger. Hurt. No more lies.
No lonely child that sits and cries.
A friendly world that's calm and fair.
No more arguments, everyone shares.
So hope and pray and maybe one day,
This simple daydream will become reality.

Holly Hayward (14)
Kingsbrook School, Milton Keynes

The World

The moaning,
Groaning,
Whines of voices
Imagine
The world without pain
I dream of this world, I dream of a world,
A world without
Racism
Disease
Or prejudice
We drown in the ice of sadness
We parade in the shadow of injustice
This should not happen!
The world should have no fear
No racism
No disease

One day this may happen
One day the world will be whole!

Ryan Setter (13)
Kingsbrook School, Milton Keynes

The War

Destruction, death.
A ruined childhood.
Scared by bombs and the friends that died.
She lay in her bed, tossing and turning
Wishing her dad was back home.
Her frightened fists clutched together
As the deafening bombs struck in the sky.
She had a dream, that night,
Where the whole world lived in a declaration of peace.
Nobody was hurt, nobody had the right to kill
And most importantly her dad was back home.

Stephanie Green (13)
Kingsbrook School, Milton Keynes

I Have A Dream

I have a dream that everybody's equal.
I have a dream that no one is in poverty.
I have a dream that people aren't at war.
I have a dream that people aren't dying.

In my dream everything was made fair
There were no Third World countries
There were no dangerous places or people
There were no sins or sadness.

In my dream people were peaceful
There wasn't global warming
There weren't any terrorists
There wasn't disease or sickness.

I had a dream that everyone was equal
I imagined everything was perfect
But people are at war
But people are in poverty
But people are dying.

Alasdair Bell-Ashe (14)
Kingsbrook School, Milton Keynes

Blue Skies

People always say,
'The grass is greener on the other side.'
Well I'm telling you, it's not!
I've been there, done that
And I even got the T-shirt
And now all I see is . . .
Blue skies dreaming of rainy days
Mascara dreaming to be lip liner
White and black dreaming of each other.
I've seen a lot in my time and all I've learned
Is that when you do eventually find 'the other side' . . . you'll regret it!
My dream is that everyone will have such happiness
There will be no need for the other side.
He dreams and she dreams in the dead of night of 'the other side'.
And in their old age, when they have been,
They will regret it because they took for granted what they kept dearest
Love and passion aspiring down to greed.
But knowing there is still hope!

Amber Cole-Pendrey (13)
Kingsbrook School, Milton Keynes

There Once Was A Time . . .

There once was a time when war was thought to be foolish,
There once was a time when suffering and pain never existed,
There once was a time when hunger and poverty was impossible,
There once was a time when people would talk things over rather
than shout and argue,
There once was a time when the world was generally a better place,
But could it ever be like this again?
Is it possible?

Ryan Scannell (14)
Kingsbrook School, Milton Keynes

War

Off we go to war
Load your gun
Have no fun
Sitting in the trench
With Uncle Bun
And his gun

Bang, bang, bang!
The sound of the gun
Bang, bang, bang!
The war has been won
Bang, bang, bang!
We've done what we've done.

We killed so many
It is so sick
Just shooting away
That's the problem with today
And that's the story of the war today.

Bradley Reynolds (15)
Kingsbrook School, Milton Keynes

Space

I gazed upon the stars one day,
thinking, what was out there beyond them?

All I could see were planets floating around in space
and space shuttles on the moon.

With the moon shining so bright and the stars glimmering
beyond the sky
with those astronauts flying by in those hovering space rockets
going at the speed of light.

Ciaran Martin (14)
Kingsbrook School, Milton Keynes

Split Personality

When I get to school she's there,
When I go to class, she's there.

She writes on the tables,
She draws in our books,
She's a bully, but she's always there.

She sits on the foot of my bed,
I want her to get out of my head!
She's a bully,
But she's always there!

Where did she come from?
How did it get like this?
I thought we were friends!
I thought we were one!
But I was wrong!

The bully is me!
Is a bully really what I want to be?

Katie Gallop (12)
Kingsbrook School, Milton Keynes

Change

I hear a cry,
There is a starved child.

There is a sobbing mother,
Weeping for her child.

A bomb explodes,
I see crimson sand.

Is this real or fantasy?

This can be fantasy,
This can be stopped.

We can change.

James Griffiths (11)
Kingsbrook School, Milton Keynes

Dream World

As I go and rest my head
As I go to sleep in my bed
I see a vision in the night
A vision I know is right

Small children playing in the sand
All helping each other, hand in hand
Peace rules over us for evermore
War is now a burden, a chore

Tears that fall now come from laughter
This is the human race's happy ever after
Martin Luther King would be happy to see this day
His children and others gone out to play

As this dream world starts to fade
This world I have made
I awake in this world full of hate
And I think of a world full of joy, how long do I have to wait?

James Barclay (14)
Kingsbrook School, Milton Keynes

Greed

Do you ever think about what you have?
Or just what you want?
Do you give thanks for the food you receive
Or just take it and waste it?

People starve with no shelter
But you want a new TV or a bigger house
Do you put money in the charity box?
Or just walk away, selfish and cross
You can solve the problem but choose not to
You can stop the starving but don't
You can shelter them but don't.
Why?

Devan Patel (12)
Kingsbrook School, Milton Keynes

I Have A Dream

Martin Luther King who had a dream,
the red, red rose of victory,
he who was right,
he who rose as a brother, a saver,
helper to all of the black people.
It took a lot and I respect him for that,
and justice,
and freedom,
for his family, children of all colours,
to hold hands and be one,
and together rise because he had a dream.

And he knew,
knew he'd do it for all it took,
for the brilliant human race,
but for what he believed, was shot.
So rest in peace he will, and a dream.

Natasha Lyman (11)
Kingsbrook School, Milton Keynes

A Dream World

There are many types of dreams.
Good ones, bad ones, many about past, some about present
And future dreams about the world.
I had a dream that global warming was just a myth.
I had a dream that the world was at peace and
Conflict was no more.
I had a dream that poverty was a scheme to make
Large sums of money.
I had a dream but I'm not sure that it will
Ever,
Ever,
Ever
Come true.

Connor Murphy (14)
Kingsbrook School, Milton Keynes

Untitled And Unwanted

We look at criminals like they are dirt,
But they're secretly deprived.
Lonely behind a brave face they hurt,
Shocked they've so far survived.
Their face like a mask,
One of violence and hatred.
Their lives seem like an endless task,
Their identity must be kept sacred.
So there was one man who believed,
Believed they could all be equal.
They were admired, and felt relieved,
They hoped for a sequel.
Another chance even,
A chance, to be completely reborn.
To be in a life undeceiving,
Without contempt scorn.

Ellen Cooke (12)
Kingsbrook School, Milton Keynes

Sleepyhead

I sleep all night under the moon
I sleep all morning until noon
I doze on the chair
Without any care
Sleeping my life away
I snore in my bed
I'm a real sleepyhead!
I sleep in the car
When we travel quite far
Even sleep at the fair
But I just don't care!
I'm sleeping my life away.
What a waste of time!

Jonathan Hand (11)
Kingsbrook School, Milton Keynes

Love, Life And Death

I remember that day
When my woes went away
His eyes sparkled at mine
My smile was as wide as a Cheshire cats.

Everything about him drew me in,
His smile, his laugh, his scent. All I wanted
Was to be in his presence, to me he was royalty.

Many months past, nothing's changed
My love for him will last,
Whilst I admire from my shadow . . .

At night he cries
Remembering how I died
And wishing that he'd said, 'I love you.'

Now I'm just a memory, about to be forgotten.

Katie Fulker (15)
Kingsbrook School, Milton Keynes

Poverty Poem

People just don't care,
They could donate
To the tragic
But they spend their money on crap,
They never think of others,
Especially poverty all over
This wonderful world,
People dying,
People laughing,
With not a care in the world.
Others are saving our world
As if it were their own,
But not enough,
As poverty is all over.

Joe Fitzgerald (12)
Kingsbrook School, Milton Keynes

Poverty!

Children are crying,
While their parents are dying
And all we do
Is watch TV and eat fast food.

They sit there at night,
With horror and fright,
They lie there and shake,
Will they ever awake?

No food, no drink
So weak they can't blink,
Then us, we have loads,
So fat we can't even see our toes.

So just sit, just think,
Should life have turned out like this?

Isobel Steel (11)
Kingsbrook School, Milton Keynes

Dreams

Follow your dream
don't let them go
down the stream
there she blows
set your mind free
and never let go

high, low, left, right
look for the light
when you reach
for your dreams
it will come to you
anything is possible
if you put your
mind to it.

Janelle Gray (14)
Kingsbrook School, Milton Keynes

Racism

The sky was not bright
There was a lot of fright
People were crying
People were dying.

Then came the Saviour
With good behaviour
He extinguished the crying
He stopped the dying.

Saw the sights
And got them rights
The nights were safer
And the days brighter.

So learn from Him
And don't turn from Him.

Elliot Langham (12)
Kingsbrook School, Milton Keynes

I Have A Dream!

Hugs, hearts and happiness
Songs, smiles and speech
I wish the world would be a perfect place.
Arguing, disagreeing and gossiping.
Bullying, fighting, cheating.
We live in a cynical world.
Every day hundreds of people wake up
Scared or anxious for some reason.
Is this what the world should be like?
Express your feelings truthfully
But don't make them harsh.
The wars should stop and we should all make peace.
I believe this would get rid of the violence
And everyone should be happy.

Frankie Baldwin (14)
Kingsbrook School, Milton Keynes

My Dream Is The World's Dream

I have a dream.
War. Overtaken by peace and is no longer an opportunity.
Race. Look through the colours of our skin.
Safety. Our curiosity of the contents in our inky, dark streets
will be forgotten.
Poverty. Communism to be banished and to stop taking
the lives of the young.
Pain. Life swells up with fear, uncertainty and shock.
Judgement. To express our feeling verbally, without locking
up our negative emotions.
Drugs. Get high on life and not the narcotics rotting
in our bloodstream.
My dream is the world's dream
And I soon hope that dream will become an achievement
I can look back on.

Abigail Sullivan (14)
Kingsbrook School, Milton Keynes

I Have A Dream

I had a dream,
I had a dream that recycling became a part of everyone's life,
That children and teenagers stopped carrying a knife,
I had a dream that litter didn't line the street,
That food for Third World countries wasn't a treat,
I had a dream that bullying stopped in everyone's school,
That animal testing ended when people realised it was cruel,
I had a dream that the world became a better place,
That fighting stopped and problems were sorted face to face,
I had a dream that abuse stopped in every home,
That starving children weren't just skin and bone,
I had a dream that war stopped
And peace started.
I have a dream.

Rebecca Garratt (15)
Kingsbrook School, Milton Keynes

Can You Believe?

Can you run the fastest mile, or sail the roughest sea?
Or climb the highest peak, or tame the wildest beast?
Yes you can if you just believe, it's not that hard, just try.

Have you ever seen a star that shines so bright?
The one you always wish on and always speak your mind.
But why do you do this and give it so much faith?
You just know that you believe.

Are you that falling star?
Are you the special one?
Are you going to change your life?
Are you the one who's always in the crowd, changing, changing your life?
Yes you are, yes you're the one.
You can do anything you want to, if you believe so.
Can you believe?

Olivia Flannery (13)
Kingsbrook School, Milton Keynes

The Deathly Kiss

Every 3 seconds I click
A mosquito makes its pick
Every 3 seconds someone dies
Some due to the deadly bug that flies
We can stop this with a mosquito net
That will stop the Devil's pet
All it takes is a bit of money
Well is that funny?
I believe we can do this
We can stop the bug's kiss
So reach into your pocket
Don't let more lives kick the bucket
Please help me in my pledge
We can do this.

Jack Thorpe (12)
Kingsbrook School, Milton Keynes

Child Abuse

She walks to school with her messy hair,
Wearing the same dress she wore yesterday,
She shows the pain behind the mask
They never ask, no one knows the pain.

She screams,
She shouts,
The neighbours pretend
And they turn out the light.

She goes to bed
With her hope and bravery
Holding her teddy bear,
He is the only one,
He knows the pain behind the mask.

Harriet Millar (12)
Kingsbrook School, Milton Keynes

Friends

Friends are there to help
Imagine if they didn't
Friends should always help
Forget them if they hate you

You may only get one shot at friendship
So don't waste it
Whether older or younger
They're always there for you

Friends are like family
Brothers and sister
Count on them for a laugh
You won't be disappointed.

David Standring (12)
Kingsbrook School, Milton Keynes

My Love Lol!

I wake up and think of you,
I really don't know what to do.
You're a true mate,
And I think you're absolutely great.

You have such lustrous hair,
Especially when it's in the air.
Sometimes you're colourful,
And I think it's wonderful.

I would run a mile,
Just for your lovely smile.
I would love to be there
Or else my heart would tear.

Brandon Proctor (13)
Kingsbrook School, Milton Keynes

Why Me

You see people you wish you could be like,
You see people you want to be,
You see others who get abused by their family,
Why does it have to be me?

You see people who have nice clothes,
You see people who have nice hair,
You see others who dance and jump for glee,
Why is it never me?

You see people who have loads of friends,
You see people who are a teacher's pet,
You see others who sit and play with their tie,
Why do I sit there and cry?

Laura Stefanovic (12)
Kingsbrook School, Milton Keynes

Terrified

I stood there in the pouring rain,
crying and crying in so much pain.
Wondering when he was coming home,
feeling shut out and all alone.
I then started to put on one of my tents,
feeling so afraid in such torment.

The sound of the creak gave me a fright,
he walked through the door and turned on the light,
in a blink of an eye I was lying on the ground,
feeling so terrified with the quietest sound.

Gripping so tight to my little tatty bear,
just wishing and wishing that someone would care.

Isabella White (12)
Kingsbrook School, Milton Keynes

I Have A Dream

Trees sway in the mid-summer breeze
Many different types as far as the eye can see
The lake is still and silent
Filled with frogs and fish
Fishermen wait at the water's edge
With no industry to disturb
The peacefulness of the world.
This is my dream, this is my only wish
For the world to be a better place
Before happiness is laid to waste.
War and misery are a thing of the past
All the bad things will not last.

Matthew Pitcher (13)
Kingsbrook School, Milton Keynes

Louise's Dream!

I have a dream that people don't suffer from illness.
I have a dream that people *don't* die.
I have a dream that children *don't* get abused.
I have a dream that drug addicts stay off drugs.
I have a dream that homeless people have a house.
I have a dream that rapes, murders and burglaries don't exist.
I have a dream that guns and knives are abolished.
I have a dream that electricity doesn't ever run out,
I have a dream that people keep the environment healthy.
I have a dream that our past freezes like a picture.
I have a dream that days are longer.
I have a dream that the ones that have conditions *don't* hide away.
I have a dream that disabled people shouldn't be locked up when people stare.
I have a dream that people accept who we are.
I have a dream that swine flu would end.
I have a dream that there are no racial comments ever again.

Louise McDonough (13)
Lonsdale School, Stevenage

The World In Dreaming

D omestic violence would come to an end.
R oyal people would be a bit more humane.
E nding knife crime will be made reality.
A busing children comes to a full stop.
M any people would be named and shamed.
I njured people would get the care needed.
N eglect would be finished with.
G oodness gracious, that's a lot of dreaming.

Callum Dixon (14)
Lonsdale School, Stevenage

My Dream

D own under the sky every night, millions of homeless people are lying in the street with nowhere to go and no money of their own. My dream is that these people have a place to go and a family of their own.

R emember that every day hundreds of children are being abused. My dream is that all children will have a happy and loving family to live with.

E very day there are many families being torn apart by family members being taken to war. My dream is that there will be no wars and so many people will still have their lives.

A nyone can be killed by a knife or a gun, but just remember how the families will feel after losing them. My dream is that there will be no knife crime and that everyone in this world will live with each other in peace.

M y dream!

Chrystal Hendry (14)
Lonsdale School, Stevenage

Stop Cruelty To Children

I have a dream:
That cruelty to children will stop.
I have a dream:
That children won't be scared
To go home after school.
I have a dream:
That children will speak out
Without fear of retribution!
I have a dream:
That children will stop being abused!

Ted Ryan (14)
Lonsdale School, Stevenage

Dreams Of The World

I have a dream;
That knife crime will stop and no person ever
gets killed by a knife. *Don't use a knife!*
Please make a change!

I have a dream;
In this world too many children are getting
abused and hurt. *Don't abuse children!*
So please make a change!

I have a dream;
Too many people are drink driving
People are getting killed and maimed.
Don't drink and drive.
So please make a change!

Kevin Harris (11)
Lonsdale School, Stevenage

The Dream

I have a dream
That no one will die from swine flu
I hope it will not attack you
I have a dream
That all wars should end
And everyone will be your friend
Remember, we have love to send
I have a dream to stop children getting hurt
Free from poverty and living in dirt.

Marcus Gomez (15)
Lonsdale School, Stevenage

A Dream About My Family

I have a dream
Across the stream
I believe in my family
Across the stream
I have a dream
That all my family will be happy forever
I hope that all my family can swim across the stream.

Shannon Cooper (16)
Lonsdale School, Stevenage

Respect

D egrading is so overated
R espect is the key
E xpectation is the answer
A nger is not the way
M aking pain is no one's gain.

Danny Grint (16)
Lonsdale School, Stevenage

I Have A Dream

I have a dream to change my looks
Every day
I have a dream to get a rich boyfriend
I have a dream
That could change my life
And free me from all strain and strife.

Sam Charalambous (15)
Lonsdale School, Stevenage

I Have A Dream

I look up at the starry skies
Millions shining like the sun, bursting open my eyes
If only a person was a star
Then this world would still be travelling far
If everyone could just simply recycle
Lose the cars and go out and cycle
If only the world was at peace
Slowly but strongly, piece by piece
Global warming would be a thing of the past
Everyone would be happy, having a blast
But global warming is a fire, it keeps going on and on
It takes more than one person to extinguish it before it is gone
Though someday those stars will be my crowd
Just being there, standing proud
A dream is a dream but I want this one to become true
Please for everyone, even for you
Still I look up at the starry skies
Millions shining like the sun, bursting open my eyes.

Katie Morton (12)
Moulsham High School & Humanities College, Chelmsford

I Have A Dream

My midsummer night's dream is not that grand,
It's not for power, money or land,
It's not a 'change the world' type of thing,
Like the dream of Martin Luther King.

Or things too fantastic to be true like
Coleridge's dream of Xanadu,
My personal dream if I may,
Is to recite the Bard in a Shakespearean play.

So although I yearn for an end to war,
Of children with AIDS which I abhor,
Of poverty, abuse, anger and hate,
All things I would eliminate.

In my midsummer night's dream in an
Elizabethan doublet,
I end to applause with a rhyming couplet.

Niamh O'Leary (11)
Moulsham High School & Humanities College, Chelmsford

I Have A Dream

I have a dream . . .
To change hatred into love,
The flourishing jealousy,
The conflict between the competitors,
Into -
The tender roots,
Blossoming amongst innocent buds

I have a dream . . .
To change the divide between the social classes,
The minute gulf taking over
The democracy,
Into -
The smooth petals working as one,
As the sun sets off in the west

I have a dream . . .
To change the way we are treated,
The prejudice and abhorrence against us,
The downwards look, the spiteful comments, the gossiping
Into -
A world that judges nobody by its cover,
And instead people's actions allow us to see the light

I have a dream . . .
To change the lies being said,
The dishonesty, deceit that is said to me in hate,
Leaving me unaware, in ignorance towards the truth,
Into -
The calming scent of the lavender plant,
The sweet fragrance of . . .
Truth.

Kavita Patel (15)
Newlands Girls' School, Maidenhead

I Have A Dream . . .

(Inspired by the King of Freedom and the King of Pop)

Now is the time to change the world,
End war let peace reign,
We can never be satisfied until there is a change,
I have a dream that one day
The world will live in harmony,
Let freedom ring from war grounds
To churches quiet and still.

Now is the time to make a difference,
Speak your mind, don't refrain,
We can never be satisfied until there is a change,
I have a dream one day all people will have a say,
Let freedom ring on Independence Day.

Now is the time to stop all crime,
Death is not a game,
We can never be satisfied until there is a change,
I have a dream one day all people will be safe,
Let freedom ring from face to face.

Now is the time to end homelessness,
This should be our aim,
We can never be satisfied until there is a change,
I have a dream one day all people
Will have a sheltered place,
Let freedom ring for the human race.

Now is the time to see real change,
Look in the mirror and make that change,
We can be satisfied if we fulfil our dreams,
Let freedom ring so we can live our dreams.

Carina Panchal (11)
St Albans Girls' School, St Albans

How Do We Get Dreams?

How do we get dreams?
They appear out of the blue,
We close our eyes and there they are,
But here's the secret truth.

Dreams are made by aliens
Who insert them in our ears,
They're there to keep us entertained,
By humour and our fears.

You may not like your dreams,
But you really should,
They stop us dying from boredom,
Who knew you ever could?

So when you wake up in the night,
Because you had a nightmare,
Remember dreams are life saving,
You would die if they weren't there!

Holly George-Samuels (12)
St Albans Girls' School, St Albans

My Life

Life is a flow of constant changes
Starting from existence in my mother's womb
Blooming with hopeful life
Depending on which way I choose to go
Not knowing what is around the corner
Life is but a mystery
Taking family for granted
Which could be just a memory tomorrow?
Every day is a new challenge
But I will learn to adjust
As I want to make the best of my life
As we only have one life to live.

Hannah Ward (11)
The Billericay School, Billericay

Helen Adams Keller

She is an inspiration,
To almost everyone I know.
She was blind and she was deaf,
But still she gave her very best.

She was an American author,
Of books you may not know.
And who knows how she wrote them,
I have been thinking so.

Her teacher called Anne Sullivan,
She helped her get this far,
Once she was known worldwide,
I'm sure that she couldn't hide.

Although her death's a shame,
I'm sure she played her game.
Gave us all her very best,
To help others with such a zest.

You may not have known,
What I've just told you so.
It's a shame she isn't here today,
To learn, laugh, sing and play.

She was a great doctor,
Probably a great patient too.
But she is still equal
To both me and you.

Although she was disabled
And isn't here today.
I'm sure that we can prove to her
We're worthy of what we see
And hear today.

Rebecca Hopkins (12)
The Billericay School, Billericay

The World And Me

I look out my bedroom window
To see such wonderful views,
The birds, trees and meadows
And the sky so turquoise blue.

I know I am so lucky
To breathe in fresh clean air,
I live in so much comfort
And I have no cares.

People indifferent countries
Lacking food and things,
I wish I had more money,
Millions to do lots of different things like
Buy food, clothes and water and
Adopt a little child, open up my arms and
Shout, 'Come here and live in my land.'

My view gives me inspiration
To try to be a better me,
'Cause one day soon I will be happy
To help people who have less than me.

McKenzie Pickering (12)
The Billericay School, Billericay

Inspirational Poem

You can follow your dreams
Any day of the year
Whatever it is
Even if it is queer.

Follow your hero and
Let them take the lead
Get the help you need to get
To help you succeed.

It could be a challenge
That could be very hard
But if you think positively
You're sure to go far.

Life is sometimes difficult
Attempt your goal in every way
It may seem unachievable
But you could do it
By the end of the day.

Georgia Chevalier (11)
The Billericay School, Billericay

Here's To The Kids

Here's to the kids
Here's to the kids who sit there day after day
Who sit there alone only turning round to see strangers.
Here's to the kids who put up with sitting at the table,
Or in their shared bedrooms and still no one to turn to.

Here's to the kids
Who are worth more than being chucked in a home.
Here's to the kids who some have forgotten.
Here's to the kids who suffer abuse,
The kids whose cries are never heard,
Here's to the kids who deserve more.

Emma Girdlestone (12)
The Billericay School, Billericay

Iraq War

I have a dream that one day this mass murder will end
And that those families that have lost a member
Will be relieved for no one else will suffer.

I have a dream that cultures
Will one day
Live in harmony and not misery.

I have a dream

I have hope that one day
We can bring our warriors home
Who have survived the carnage.

I have a hope that
I could fly into Iraq and not have an assassination attempt.
I hope that I could fly into Iraq and get cheers.

I have a dream that
The world will be in peace!

James Newton (11)
The Billericay School, Billericay

War & Peace

In the eyes of war there is only blood,
In the eyes of peace there is only hope,
In the head of war there is only confusion,
In the head of peace there is only a rope,
To take those hurt and pull them up.

In the hands of war there is only hate,
In the hands of peace there is only pain,
In the heart of war there is only fate
In the heart of peace there is only a mate,
To cheer people up and make them laugh and cry.

Max Johnston (11)
The Billericay School, Billericay

I Will

I believe we should have a right to keep secrets.
I believe we should have a right
To express our feelings in ways we want.
I believe we should have a right to let things out.
I believe, I believe, I believe.

I hope we will learn from our mistakes
And make the world a better place.
I hope I die before my friends and family.
I hope my dad can get out of hospital
I hope, I hope, I hope.

I will learn from my mistakes and
Make my world a better place.
I will keep secrets
I will express my feelings however I want
I will let it out
I will, I will, I will.

William Cummings (12)
The Billericay School, Billericay

Untitled

Will fight for country
Will fight for queen
Will fight for our families
Will fight for our lives
Will fight for peace.

Robson Redding (12)
The Billericay School, Billericay

The Soldiers Of WWI & II

They were very brave,
They risked their lives,
They used weapons
Like guns and knives.
Sometimes their families
Didn't see them again,
Because they were killed,
Those men.
They went through pain,
They went through suffering,
When they got hurt, they weren't bluffing.
So here is a message from them to you,
Stay out of fights,
Be safe and be careful
Whatever you do!

Ailish Murphy (12)
The Billericay School, Billericay

Untitled

I'm happy to be alive.
I'm happy to be me
The dreams of moons and stars and
All the things I can be.

The lapping shores
And the crystal clear water
Staring at me
All the dreams I have
And of everything I can be.

Bright horizon, the sun and the moon
Watching the cars zoom
All the dreams I have
And everything I can be.

Katie Brewer (11)
The Billericay School, Billericay

Make A Change

I believe that we have a right to let things out
I believe that we should be able to express things
I believe that we can do anything if we have hope

I hope that we can get through all of the stress
I hope that we can get through all of this pain
I hope that this will end soon

I will try to be a better person
I will try to be kind to people more
I will try to be good to my mother

I can be normal to everyone if I try
I can sleep at night if I try
I can walk to school and talk to friends if I try.

Connor Hatch (11)
The Billericay School, Billericay

I Believe

I believe
I can be successful
I can do anything I want or need to do,
And I can support my friends
Like they have done for me
My friends are always supportive
And they will be there till the end.
They have helped me through hard times,
Without them
I wouldn't have even thought
Of doing any of the things
I have now done.
My friends, my everything.

Rachael Jobling (12)
The Billericay School, Billericay

I'm Free

The patient stood under a
Silent spell of deep sleep.
Distant screams and sirens were heard.
Mysterious shadows darted and crept.
Apart from that, everything
Untouched, nothing disturbed.

The chimes of a clock cried,
Midnight had come.
A crooked old figure soon emerged,
Moving gracefully not making a sound.
This may be the answer I thought:
Well it is for some.
He moved towards me and
Held out the packet, cackling aloud.

The world turned dark,
I felt alone, I started to shake.
Depressed, sad, lonely, nobody around.
My whole home around me
Started to break.
My family leaving, I wasn't myself.

The Devil's sky lightened,
Sun shining on my face.
Happiness surrounded me,
I couldn't help but smile.
No sign of sorrow and alienation
In this perfect place.
I felt an achievement,
A goal had been scored,
Like my life had been worthwhile.

The crooked man appeared before my eyes,
Still wearing the evil smirk.
He shook the powdery white stuff
Impatiently at me.

But I was smarter, one step ahead.
I gave my head a little jerk.
I shook my head and pushed him away;
I knew I was free.

Rebecca Evans (13)
The Cornwallis Academy, Maidstone

Why Smoke?

What's the point?
Sure, you may look cool at the time
But look 20 years down the line,
Those moments you wish you could keep, gone forever.
That one decision is 10 years of your life.

Don't do it says everyone else,
Listen to them you may think you know best
But really you're scared, worried and unsure what to do,
Is it your friend encouraging you?
Stop and think what sort of friend is that
That is trying to take 10 years off your life.

Just think before you make that one decision,
Think of all the things that could happen
If you made the right decision
And think of everything that would happen
If you made the wrong decision.

Maybe you made that wrong decision, trying to put it right?
Just stop. Yes it will be hard
But if you want it that bad, it's not going to be easy.
Keep away from the crowds of smokers and keep focused.
You know that's not the life you want anymore.

You know what the way forward is
And you know what you have to do.
So don't start smoking
And if you made the wrong decision, you know what to do.

Carly Peacock (12)
The Cornwallis Academy, Maidstone

My Inspirational Poem

If you feel mad
Don't be scared.
There is always another day,
Just walk away.

If you're upset.
It will make the pillow wet.
There is always another day.
Just walk away.

When I go to lunch.
I will always have a munch.
People give me a punch.
Just walk away.

When I get a punch.
I will have my heart in pain.
It will make you feel sorry.
Just walk away.

Ask the bully what the problem is.
And see if we can sort it out.
Don't have any doubt.
Just walk away.

Verse 6
Find someone to talk to.
A teacher or a friend.
They will help you until the end.
Just walk away.

I am a target for the bully.
They all think my name is Molly.
They don't like me, I'm always jolly.
Just walk away.

I have a friend who is a bully.
I always get picked on by Holly.
She thinks I'm shy, but I don't lie.
It makes me cry.
Just walk away.

Katie Parker (12)
The Cornwallis Academy, Maidstone

Problems

I went to lunch and I got a punch
My stomach really hurts,
Tomorrow is another day
Forget the bullies, walk away.

Later on I went for a walk to the supermarket
I saw them hiding in a corner and decided to park it!
Tomorrow is another day
Forget the bullies, walk away.

I decided to see through the light,
Stand up for myself,
I went up to the bullies and put my fear away
Tomorrow is another day,
Forget the bullies, walk away.

I told them I'd had enough, sick and tired of it
They told me they would leave me be,
So I walked away
Tomorrow is another day
Forget the bullies, walk away.

Now that I am free
I have no further problems,
Today is another day
I forgot the bullies and walked away.

Joshua Cockett (13)
The Cornwallis Academy, Maidstone

Bullying

Bullies make your life pure hell,
Let it out in one big yell,
Think about this every day,
Ignore the bullies, walk away.

If you don't know what to do,
Don't think about bullies, think of you,
Stop the feelings then just say,
Ignore the bullies, walk away.

If you go to break with no lunch,
And see the bullies in one big bunch,
They say, 'Give me your lunch,' every day,
Ignore the bullies, walk away.

If they beat you up after school,
Don't worry about bullies, just stand tall,
Just stand by, it will be okay,
Ignore the bullies, walk away.

If you walk to school or get the bus,
And see the bullies, don't make any fuss,
If they blame you about things you say,
Ignore the bullies, walk away.

If you go to bed and dream about them,
And can't get to sleep until half ten,
Change your dream In every way,
Ignore the bullies, walk away.

Think about this poem, hear me out,
Now be calm and please don't shout,
Remember this every day
Ignore the bullies, walk away.

Amie Freeman (13)
The Cornwallis Academy, Maidstone

At The Starting Gates!

At the starting gates
My heart is beating a mile a minute
At the starting gates
I imagine the trophy at the finish
As the gates open
My horse lunges forward
At the race track in Crowford
The sound of hoof beats
Like a mambo rhythm
The silk on my top slithers through the wind
As we near the first corner
I overtake into first
I use my speed in short bursts
Looking behind, number 12 is on my tail
But every race I enter, I never fail
Along the straight, I whip my horse on
The straight seems so long
Number 12 comes up alongside me
But I get free
I cross the line and win by a hoof
As I lift the trophy the crowd raises the roof
I smile for my photo, proud I have won again
With my prize money, I'm off to Spain!

Freya Harris (12)
The Cornwallis Academy, Maidstone

Seasons' Power

Lightning strikes on houses and trees
Summer is coming with bumblebees
Spring, blossom, winter, frost
Seasons changing, never lost.

Hannah Stockham (13)
The Cornwallis Academy, Maidstone

On The Streets

Always scared when you're on the streets,
Be brave, hold your head up high,
Cold and pale as you lay,
Don't give up, you'll find a way,
So many people just walk by,
Without giving another thought.

Every day feels like forever,
For now you find it hard,
Gather your things and you'll be gone,
Having the life that you dreamed of,
Though for now, hold your head up high.

In the town people are shouting,
Just as you're trying to get to sleep,
Kindness doesn't come at night,
Just try and be strong,
It will all be yours one day.

So hold your head up high,
It may be bad,
But soon you'll be in a nice warm bed,
Just try and be strong,
And hold your head up high!

Katie Bishop (13)
The Cornwallis Academy, Maidstone

The Trees Are Swaying

The trees are swaying from side to side
The flowers are blooming in the bright light
The sea is shining in the sun's glowing rays
This is the world that God made.

Jessica Sheppard (12)
The Cornwallis Academy, Maidstone

An End To Bullying Worries

When you're bullied, feeling sad,
And you don't know how you will cope.
Tell someone to make you feel glad,
Instead of just having to hope.

If people are ruining your day,
Because of things they do.
Try to stay very far away,
And make sure your friends do to.

When bullies are getting you down,
And you're not sure what to do.
Tell someone to help and fix your frown,
Then happiness will come to you.

Now you know what exactly to do,
When bullies get in your way.
I am sure you will not feel sad and blue,
But instead have a brilliant day.

Nicole Fowler (13)
The Cornwallis Academy, Maidstone

Believe

Believe
The fighting in Iraq would stop and terrorism would stop.
Believe
The soldiers would come home and see their family's faces.
Believe
That one voice in a crowd could change everything
And that one voice could be you.
I stand here before you
Not to brag but to say one word
Believe
Let that voice be you.

Sam Witt (13)
The Cornwallis Academy, Maidstone

3:00pm

School is over, it's time to go home,
I feel unhappy but I don't want to moan.

I open the door filled with dread,
I hope my mum is tucked up in bed.

I'm meant to feel safe in my own home,
But really I don't: I feel alone.

Sometimes I feel she doesn't care,
And then I begin to feel despair.

I hope she hasn't been drinking again,
'Cause when she does I feel so much pain.

She will start to shout and scream at me,
And once again I'll get no tea.

Why does she have to do this to me?
I think her life's a catastrophe.

I dream that one day my mum will be well,
But if she keeps drinking you never can tell.

Jessica Hillyard (13)
The Cornwallis Academy, Maidstone

Untitled

Paige is my name
Football is my game
I support the Arsenal
Cos they are so cool
I play in red for Soccer Elite
It's so much fun - I love to compete
I play right back in matches we play
My favourite games are the ones away
Maybe one day I'll play for Arsenal
I'll make my mum proud by playing football.

Paige Daniels (13)
The Cornwallis Academy, Maidstone

My Inspiring Poem

Loads of people need some food
Even if they're in quite a mood
Lots of people have no phone
And worst of all no nice, big home
Help the poor and the needy
Give some money, don't be greedy

There could be a man whose name is Pete
Who might only want a piece of meat
After walking the streets all day
He might just want a place to stay
Help the poor and the needy
Give some money, don't be greedy

Come on now and help them
Even if your name is Ken
Go on please be kind
Even if they've lost their mind
Help the poor and the needy
Give some money, don't be greedy.

Scott Coombs (13)
The Cornwallis Academy, Maidstone

Stand Up Tall

Even though they make you feel all alone,
Insignificant, small and sad,
Remember that you never have to cope on your own,
Because inside your shell it will drive you mad.

So do not be depressed, stand up tall
Forget the bullies even exist,
Tell your friends or a teacher, that's all,
There's another thing off your list.

Annabel Harris (12)
The Cornwallis Academy, Maidstone

What Am I?

I am red, I'm black, I'm yellow,
In fact I'm any colour . . .
What am I?

I go out in any weather;
Rain, snow, sunshine . . .
What am I?

You see me every day,
But you don't notice me . . .
What am I?

I am used every day,
And frequently thrown away . . .
What am I?

I've been banned from many places,
But I have not got an ASBO . . .
What am I?

If I'm not looked after and discarded carelessly,
I will destroy your world . . .
What am I?

I'm just a plastic bag!

Georgia Martin (12)
The Cornwallis Academy, Maidstone

To Be Me

My friends say
You have to act a certain way
Pretend to be proud
And follow the crowd

This makes me feel
That life seems unreal
I want to be free
I want to be me

Breaking free
And being me
Seems to be
The best thing

No need to hide
What's inside
I can see everything's
Alright.

Sian Smith (12)
The Cornwallis Academy, Maidstone

Alcohealth

Alcohol may be nice but think about your health,
Do you really want to get addicted?
It alters your mind, you become Jekyll and Hyde
Why are you drinking, what are you thinking?

You're harming yourself and everyone else,
You're lying and scheming and deceiving yourself,
You've got no money and you've got no friends,
Why are you drinking, what are you thinking?

Think about getting your confidence back,
Not being down in the dumps,
Think about having a clear mind and getting on with your life,
Why are you drinking, what are you thinking?

You can get help,
Don't be scared,
Just talk to someone who can help,
Why are you drinking, what are you thinking?

Victoria Jarvis (13)
The Cornwallis Academy, Maidstone

Untitled

So you think it's cool to be taking drugs huh?
Well, let me start you off with a little something.
Hit it
You think about drugs at a very young age,
Same as a book; what's on the next page?
You turn it over and life's like Hell,
You see your friends with drugs to sell.
In your world you're out at school,
Where you 'have' to take drugs to be so 'cool'.
So, drop them drugs and get out and about,
Your life will be better . . . without a doubt.

Catherine Holmes (13)
The Cornwallis Academy, Maidstone

Teenagers And Drugs!

Want to buy some drugs?
They can be fun,
I've got uppers, downers, weed and speed,
Do some drugs!

No thanks I don't do drugs,
I don't want to wreck my life,
I'll get my highs elsewhere,
Don't do drugs!

But where else will you get the buzz?
From all the stuff I've got stashed,
Try this for free, go on,
Do some drugs!

I just said *no,* don't need that,
I have *big* plans for my life,
That don't include your stuff,
Don't do drugs!

Lara Jackson (12)
The Cornwallis Academy, Maidstone

Bad Things

If you want to lead a happy life,
Listen to my friendly advice.
Alcohol can go to your head,
It may leave you in a hospital bed.

Smoking can damage your lungs and heart,
So don't do it and be smart.
Don't try drugs they make you ill,
Not even one because it can kill.

Amie Palmer (13)
The Cornwallis Academy, Maidstone

Another Day

Tomorrow's another day
Forget the bullies, walk away
Don't worry about it
They'll be gone tomorrow
Walk away.

Tomorrow's another day
Forget the bullies, walk away
Even though you may be scared
They may stare you down
Walk away.

Tomorrow's another day
Forget the bullies, walk away
You are better than them
You will never forget just
Walk away.

Vicky Franklin (12)
The Cornwallis Academy, Maidstone

Smoking – The Way Out

Stop the smoke,
Put out the fag,
Because if you keep on smoking,
It will ruin your life.

The smoke will make you addicted,
It will make you want it even more,
You need to stop,
Before it's too late.

If you want to be smoke free,
And walk down the street
Without having to have a cigarette,
Then you must seek help,
Or it might damage your health severely.

Neville King (13)
The Cornwallis Academy, Maidstone

Put Down The Guns!

Put down the guns before it's too late
Put down the guns, don't give in to hate
Put down the guns, stop all the pain
Put down the guns and stop terror's reign

Don't try to fight
It just adds to fright
Send love not troops
Launch doves not bombs

War is the wrong way to go
Peace will steal the show
Form an alliance of trust
Don't kill out of lust

Put down the guns
Believe in friendship.

Ryan Horton (13)
The Cornwallis Academy, Maidstone

Wouldn't You Love To . . .

Wouldn't you love to . . .
Skate around the world with Tony Hawks,
Race Lewis Hamilton,
And wrestle a crocodile with Steve Irwin?

Wouldn't you love to . . .
Score a goal against Petr Cech,
Sing with Lily Allen,
Ice dance with Torvill and Dean?

Wouldn't you love to . . .
Fly with the Red Arrows,
Walk on the moon with Buzz Aldrin,
Act a scene with Zac Efron?

I know I would!

Liam Towner (13)
The Cornwallis Academy, Maidstone

Climb The Mountain

Let's climb together
We will give it a try
It is rainy weather
But we will get by

If I get tired
Or if I should slip
By memories I'm inspired
And I'll firm up my grip

And when at last
The summit's in view
Our bond will be steadfast
My father, we two.

Bryn James (13)
The Cornwallis Academy, Maidstone

A Whole New World

Life can be hard
The world can be strange
But when you get older
The world will begin to change

You will struggle
You have to understand
That the world will not meet you
Hand for hand

But never give up
Just keep on trying
Don't walk away if you feel like crying

Listen and learn from those that know
They will show you the way to go

Always have pride in whatever you do
When they teach you at One Hundred of Hoo!

Katie Fisk (11)
The Hundred of Hoo School, Rochester

Pretty Girls

They say I'm skinny,
But I think I'm *fat,*
I look in the mirror,
And my stomach's not flat.
I look at the *pretty* girls,
I *aspire* to look like them,
Wear all the great clothes,
And get all the men.
Doctors say I *must* eat,
Or I will get ill,
A *body* like a model,
For that I would kill.
I *weigh* five stone,
I *must* lose more weight,
Obey the *Pro-Ana laws,*
The rainbow diet I hate.
'Mum I'm not hungry,'
That's what I said,
Pounds dropping off,
It's an *illness* of the head.
Mum would shout,
I would *cry,*
I lay on my bed,
Wanting to *die.*
I need *help,*
I need it now,
I don't know where,
I don't know how,
So *stop* anorexia,
And *help* people like me,
You need to understand,
Then you can *see.*

Robyn Mayes (13)
The Hundred of Hoo School, Rochester

If I Could Change The World

If I could change the world
There's one thing I would change
I would stop all the animal abuse
This is a hard thing to rearrange.

If I could change the world
There's one thing I would do
I'd make every animal safe from all the dangers
To help them through.

If I could change the world
There are many things I would change
I'd give every animal a second chance
To help them have a home.

If I could find a way
To stop animal abuse
Even though it's hard to find
But every animal deserves a second chance.

If I could change the world
There's a couple of things I would do
I'd make sure every animal
Is treated properly.

If I could rearrange the world
There are some things I would do
I'd make sure that every animal has a roof over it's head
To make them safe and warm.

If you could change the world
What would you do?

Alex Higgins (12)
The Hundred of Hoo School, Rochester

Forgotten Love

You look outside and see the world around you
Covered by a blinding light
People living their daily lives each day
But do you ever think about people across the world?
What are they really feeling?
The sadness, the killing, the disastrous wars,
The fury and the tears that drop from every innocent eye.

What do you feel like now?
I can feel the shouting inside of me
The thousands of cries I can hear,
The help for survival,
The hunger of a child.
It is like an arrow has hit through my heart.
The loud beating that lingers through my mind
A single tear but from many,
A call shouting my name,
A frightened, lonely boy calling for his mother.

Lives have been forgotten
And it's like the mind has been drowned
In unhappiness, waiting to be saved.

The never forgotten faces that face me,
The feelings that are lost,
Loud noises explode and drift away.
The sea is calm as can be
Like as we are today,
Waiting patiently.

Kate Russell (14)
The Hundred of Hoo School, Rochester

Got To Get Out Of There

Story of my life
Searching for the perfect life is hard
But when you have known what some people go through
You could say that your life is pretty much perfect.

Downstairs all you can hear is screaming
Not knowing what's happening
Then everything goes silent
The door opens and you hear their footsteps
Someone weeping, screaming, 'Don't please'
Knowing that's *your* mum.

I may smile but you never know what's hiding
Behind that smile
A drunken, bullying, terrifying dad
A broken hearted, hurt, scared mum
Brothers that don't know what to do
And you crying and never going to bed like you did before.

No mum to sing you lullabies
No dad to tuck you in and kiss you goodnight
Instead my dad's half drunk and mum's downstairs crying
I have to listen to this every night.

If you think your life is bad try living mine,
Even just for a day,
Then you will know what hurt truly feels like.

Thanks for everything mum
I love you forever and always.

Hannah Kirk (13)
The Hundred of Hoo School, Rochester

My Troubled Time

My friends said 'It will be a laugh,'
So I just went along,
My heart was pounding deep inside,
I knew that it was wrong.

Now a few weeks later,
I'm doing it with ease,
I try to hide my pain away,
Breaking through boundaries.

I didn't think it would happen to me,
But somehow I just craved,
I knew I wasn't addicted,
I should have just behaved.

Rushing down to an empty hall,
My eyes all blurred and red,
People crying all around,
They thought that I was dead.

If I could have said one thing,
I would have just said, 'No,'
Drugs have brought me nothing but trouble,
I've caused so much sorrow.

My idea of a perfect world,
Would be blissful and ideal,
Everyone getting along,
If only it was real.

Rebecca Kingsley (14)
The Hundred of Hoo School, Rochester

Abuse

What has this world come to?
With rape and child abuse,
And paedophiles and animals,
The time has come to choose.

When are we going to stop this?
It's time to make a stand
If you really want to help
Please give me your hand.

Are paedophiles really good
For kids to be around them?
When I'm older, I'd really rather
Like to try and pound them!

Discrimination and rape
Why the heck do they even exist?
All the people that have been hurt
I think I'll continue my list.

Child and animal abuse
That is sick and wrong
To think of a little creature
Getting hurt or hit with a gong.

We need to try and stop this,
As you can go to jail,
You don't want a criminal record
When you're 14 and pale.

Becky Howarth & Austen Patterson (14)
The Hundred of Hoo School, Rochester

Domestic Violence

Domestic violence is a crime
Imagine being a child laying in bed scared,
Running into your brother's room holding onto
Him tight, hoping he will never let go
His hands shaking in fear.
Then you hear *crash, bang, wallop* silence,
Your mum running past you holding her face,
Slamming her bedroom door behind her,
Then your dad comes up, sitting by the door
Begging her forgiveness,
Then your dad telling you to go to bed.
In the morning you wake up,
Hoping everything's going to be OK but it never is.
You see your mum putting on a smile
But you know there is fear behind it.
A tear falls into your eye,
You try not to show you're upset but it's hard.

Imagine going through this every day.
How would you cope?
Well there are people all over the world that do,
So when you think you have it bad,
Think of people that go through this every day.

H.K this one's for you
I'm always going to be there for you.

Lydia Moore (13)
The Hundred of Hoo School, Rochester

Drugs

People think drugs are cool,
But really they're not cool at all,
There's one thing you have to remember about a drug,
After you do it you will turn into a thug.

Lloyd Buckley (15)
The Hundred of Hoo School, Rochester

Love Or Lust?

Don't lie to make me happy,
Don't lie and leave me here,
I don't need you,
Or your tainted charm,
Your feelings were false,
Your love was lust,
That made emotional harm,

I'm afraid of this loneliness,
Now our love is no longer true,
But can I stand alone,
Without you to catch me when I fall?

This disease of your affection,
Still penetrates me,
Your beauty is a virus
Attacking my veins violently.

Do not worry I'll be fine,
I'll make it through the day,
When tomorrow comes,
I hope you know,
I'll be gone,
I'll have the courage to walk away,
And it's your loss,
Because you're nothing without me.

Kirsty Marriott (14)
The Hundred of Hoo School, Rochester

Changing The World

If I had the power to change the world,
I would prevent knife crime,
This is because knife crime is rising.
Also I would change the speed limit.
I would change the limit from 70mph to 60mph.
And change 30mph to 20mph,
Because about 3 children get killed,
Every day on the London streets.

I would also try to control
The violence and racism in sports.
Too many lives are affected by violence from sports.

Illegal immigrants are another cause;
If I could control the amount of immigrants,
Everyone would be happy.
I would set a certain number
Of immigrants into the country a year.

Peace and happiness would be a treatment for depression.
Sweetness would replace the hatred
And sourness in people's' voices.
The clouds would disappear and the sun would shine on everyone.
Anger and fear would fly from this world,
And would never return.

Sophie Tarrant (14)
The Hundred of Hoo School, Rochester

Welcome To My Poems

Stop making animals die
Stop hurting children
Stop making guns
Stop hurting dogs
Change the world
Stop homework.

Scott Tomlinson (12)
The Hundred of Hoo School, Rochester

Boom Boom

Boom, boom
We're under doom
My heart is pounding,
Alarms are sounding.

Mums and dads,
Girls and lads.
Run and hide,
Make up your mind.

Boom, boom,
We're under doom.
My heart is pounding,
Alarms are sounding.

Time is running out,
There's no doubt.
Timers are short,
Three, two, one, nought.

Boom, boom,
We're under doom.
My heart is pounding,
Alarms are sounding.

Ruby Newland (14)
The Hundred of Hoo School, Rochester

My Life

I like cats
I like CBeebies
I like pollution
I like energy
I like fish
I like bullying
I don't like school
I don't like animal cruelty.

Tommy Smith (12)
The Hundred of Hoo School, Rochester

Life And Death

Life, a great thing
You take it under your wing
Death, everything goes
It all just blows.

Memories taken to places
Seeing all thoughts, faces
Bad bits of life
Things that happened to that wife.

Flowers burst into bloom
While you're beaten in a room
That mum or child
Husband or dad going wild.

You take the world on your shoulders,
All those boulders.
You won't tell 'cause it's all a blur
Or he might rape her.

But when you pick up that phone
He breaks another bone.
Now you're lying on the floor
And you're no more.

Megan Louise Prior Edwards (14)
The Hundred of Hoo School, Rochester

If Only

If only, if only I could stop hate,
All of the anger and all the rape
If only, if only I could stop fear,
And stop everyone from shedding a tear
If only, if only I could stop drugs,
And give everyone really big hugs
If only I could make the world a better place,
For the whole human race.

Connor Davidson (14)
The Hundred of Hoo School, Rochester

If Only Everyone Knew I'm Just The Same

The day starts as any should be
But not for someone who looks like me
The colour of my skin pays a fee
If only those people would leave me be.

They don't understand, no one ever lends a hand,
I wish I could float away onto my own land.

The things she says are so mean
She bullied me from 5 until a teen
The words she says don't stop going through my head
You're black, you're burnt, you're lead
You're black, you're burnt, you're lead.

The words just seem to tear my heart
If only she knew she's ripping me apart

Until the day came when I shouted 'I can't take any more.'
So I said to her,
'You're jealous of me,
So the only way is to bully me.'
So since that day she has left me be!

Alison Banin-Plockey (14)
The Hundred of Hoo School, Rochester

Why?

Why do some children drink dirty water?
Why isn't chocolate healthy?
Why are there not enough youth clubs?
Why don't we all have clear water?
Watch out for viruses
More activities, less play
We want less television
Why are the prices in the supermarket too high?

Stacey Kinslow (11)
The Hundred of Hoo School, Rochester

My Speech

For too long now I have suffered from
The violent acts of bullying but now it is high time
That I speak up about what I have had to go through
For many years of what should have been
An enjoyable school life
But unfortunately, the acts of these bullies
Ruined that time for me.

No longer will I hide because of fear.
No longer will I be threatened by cowards.
No longer will I let them ruin my life.
No longer will I not defend myself against their cruel words.
No longer will I allow them to punch,
Kick me and make me bleed
Finally, no longer will I stand back and
Allow them to crush me like an insect.

So people who are being bullied, stand up
And don't allow these bullies to ruin your life.

Maybe, after this speech I may be able to move on
And enjoy the rest of my years at school.

Luke Leaney-Sharpe (14)
The Hundred of Hoo School, Rochester

Children Of The World

This abuse' war, must end,
Unite and fight,
It will drive us around the bend,
Unless we end this fight.

We must take arm in arm,
To end this vicious war,
Watch out for their charm,
Together it will soon be over.

James Sherwood (13)
The Hundred of Hoo School, Rochester

Why So Dark?

Concrete, concrete everywhere
Trees, grass and ground now bare
This is my nightmare
But wait, I'm awake, where is the green
The green, green grass?
Why so dark?
Why so mean?
Why so flat and clean?
Why can't it be a dream?
I need to run
I need to hide
I need to get out of this mind
Now where can I go?
Where can I stay?
Where can I waste my life away?
But I can't run
I can't hide
I can't get away from this hell
I guess it's just time to die.

Danny Humberstone (15)
The Hundred of Hoo School, Rochester

Child Abuse Poem

C hange the way they think
H ow they act
I n their mind
L ove is a gift never enjoyed
D amaged physically and mentally

A bused in the mind and soul
B ullied into things they don't want to do
U nwanted in society and at home
S top their pain
E ven they don't deserve this.

Daisy Green (14)
The Hundred of Hoo School, Rochester

Army

Bodies falling to the ground.
Bullets hit them without a sound.
For our country they stand and fight.
But today might also be their last night.

Many of them injured.
Some of them are dead.
But let's think of the good things.
Not stuff we dread.

Remember ladies and gentlemen.
They are fighting for our freedom.
They are fighting for our rights.
So let's congratulate them
That they're out there night after night.

They are the best.
So they will do their best to beat the rest.
Ladies and Gentlemen, I give you the
British Army.

Ben Stirk (13)
The Hundred of Hoo School, Rochester

Terrorism

Let's all stand up against the terrorists,
They don't fight for any cause,
That is why we win the wars,
When they die their bodies fall,
And their blood splatters the wall.

Let's all unite,
And put up a fight,
Stop their crimes,
And wasting our times.
Let's not live in fear,
When we win, we shall cheer!

Christopher Bostock (13)
The Hundred of Hoo School, Rochester

Help For Heroes Acrostic Poem

H eroes help us, so why don't we help our heroes?
E ven in the battlefields their bravery lights up our world
so don't ignore.
L ove that you share for them sends guidance.
P eople, ordinary people - give their lives for yours.

F ighting through day and night, to serve their
queen and country with no disgrace.
O ne mission -
R ights for everyone, no matter what race.

H eroes of ours, so don't be blind,
E ndure death and injury for their queen and country,
through every mayhem.
R emember them, as they will remember you.
O ne mission -
E veryone they protect, we wish we could protect them.
S o sit down for a moment, and remember this poem -
help our heroes, as they would help you.

Jessie Hembery (14)
The Hundred of Hoo School, Rochester

Being Bullied

Some are different and some are the same,
So trust me, this isn't a game.

The bumps and the bruises will hurt and bring you down,
You have to fight, don't be scared and stand your ground.

Bullies are hard to handle we all know that,
So come on and cut us some slack.

The pain and the anger bottled inside us,
They make me cry they make such a fuss.

This isn't fair I've had enough,
Time to stand my ground and act real tough.

Drew Barnett (14)
The Hundred of Hoo School, Rochester

I Have A Dream

I have a dream
It floats like a boat,
It sinks when I'm angry
Or even losing my mind.

My dream
Is so scary it hides from Simon Cowell,
It is as sorrowful as a whining dog.

My dream
Feels so freaky that I cry
When I watch Children In Need,
It makes me think of
Abduction and death.

I have a dream
It floats like a boat
It sinks when I'm angry
Or even losing my mind.

Sharna Read (12)
The Hundred of Hoo School, Rochester

Black, White Or Red

I have a dream I wish it was true.
Things need to change and so do you.
Sometimes you leave me feeling so blue.
The things that you do and
The things that you say.
It really ain't the right kind of way.
May I point out, we are all the same.
Black, white or red it's all in your head.
So just for the records,
Now let it be said
That if you ain't careful,
You'll end up dead.

Kara Harwood (12)
The Hundred of Hoo School, Rochester

I Was Once A Bully

I was once a bully
Hard as nails
Didn't really care
We're just males

I was once a bully
All big and bold
Just for you
I'm not here to hold

I was once a bully
Punches like steel
Watch out!
You could be my next meal

I was once a bully
Never said 'Hi'
I was once a bully
Now it's time to say goodbye.

Samantha Brooks (15)
The Hundred of Hoo School, Rochester

Changes I Want To Happen

Poverty
Suffering
Illness
Bullying
Being sad
More wildlife
Fighting
Getting homework
Going to school
Less time at school
Rain
Longer nights.

Samara Healey (12)
The Hundred of Hoo School, Rochester

When I Got Bullied

When I got bullied
It didn't feel right
I got kicked under the table
It was such a fright.

When I got bullied
I would come home and cry
But Mummy didn't care
Because she did it as well.

When I got bullied
Home was worse
I tried to tell Daddy
But he said don't be so silly.

When I got bullied
I couldn't take no more
So I found a rope
And killed myself.

Justine Russell (13)
The Hundred of Hoo School, Rochester

If I Could Change The World

You and I will hold hands
And walk the path of brotherhood
Become united and act as one.
Remove racism, crimes and war,
Share our hopes and dreams,
Walk forward into a new day,
Ask for forgiveness and shake a hand.
Offering of peace,
Call a world summit
And create a new world,
A united world.

Jessica Okwuonu (14)
The Hundred of Hoo School, Rochester

Bullying – Now I Have A Friend

Sarah is getting bullied at school,
At lunchtime she sits all alone,
With thoughts of being in her room at home,
But then she'll only think of the hurtful things
People have said.

Jenny walks by,
She kicks Sarah intentionally,
But Sarah doesn't say anything,
She's too timid.

The next day
Lucy approached Sarah to see if she was okay,
They converse for a while then Sarah confronted Jenny,
Jenny starts to call Sarah names,
And Sarah is unhappy again.

Out of nowhere there is a *stop!*
And the bullying is ceased.

Kayleigh Anderson (13)
The Hundred of Hoo School, Rochester

What We Don't Want In The World

We all don't like pollution.
I truly don't like homework.
We all want to stop bullying.
I don't like EastEnders.
Can't we all be friends?
So stop racism.
Why do teachers give us detentions?
So stop.
I would like to stop animal cruelty.
I don't like the energy crisis.
And also the credit crunch.

David Snowden (12)
The Hundred of Hoo School, Rochester

The Feeling

I have a pulse.
I have a life.
I want to fly.
I want to soar.
I have a feeling.
There is light outside the darkness.
You can be free, you can fly.
Don't be slow to break free.
Be free.
You're not alone.
You can fly.
Just believe.
Nothing's holding you back.
Just remember we'll be there.
You can soar like an eagle.
Remember . . .
Just believe.

Rob Martin (12)
The Hundred of Hoo School, Rochester

Love And Care

Screams and cries from children at night.
No one to care,
Tell people - they don't dare.
Until one day someone sees,
What this child needs.
Love and care,
A smile and a hug,
No hatred or thugs!
Love and care,
Is what this child needs!

Keeley Don (13)
The Hundred of Hoo School, Rochester

Not Perfect

Life is black and white,
Nothing's ever right.
It's this, that or both,
You can't choose who you want to be most.
You are who you are
So you'll go far.
So just say enough is enough
So stop being rough!
You see life's a game,
Only good if you all play the same.
It's just like chess
But more of a mess.
It's now your time to go,
So remember, just say, 'No!'

I'm talking about *racism.*

Claire Mattingly (13)
The Hundred of Hoo School, Rochester

Changing The World

If I could change the world
The things I would stop are
Racism, knife crime and terrorism!
I would get rid of terrorism because
There are innocent people dying
And families are being ruined.

Knife crime needs to stop!
Little kids will get the wrong idea
And grow up to be the wrong people.

Some day racism will stop and
Black boys and black girls will
Hold hands with white boys and white girls.

Just stop it all!

Chloe Coutts (14)
The Hundred of Hoo School, Rochester

Hear My Cries

I'm growing tired of everything,
I wish he would just leave me be.
Growing weak and cold,
For what he has done to me.

Shut out from the outside world,
Not knowing what to do.
Kicking and screaming at me,
He is now slapping me hard with a shoe.

My mum couldn't say her final goodbye,
It tore me in two.
I will try hard not to cry,
Though he hurt me deep down inside.

I will never forget the emotions he has left behind,
I will never forget those people, who were so kind.

Jessica Thompson (13)
The Hundred of Hoo School, Rochester

Abuse Poem

Huddled in a corner
Thinking about her
Happy that she is
Gone forever
The sorrow and pain
Are thoughts now slain
Knowing that
She can't hurt you again
Though the scars
Can't go away
You won't see
Her another day
This is for the child that was hit
This is for the child who got through it.

Thomas Douglas (13)
The Hundred of Hoo School, Rochester

Abuse

Help me Mummy,
He's coming for me now,
He's punching me in the tummy,
And saying words that are foul.

Help me Mummy,
He's kicking me bad,
He finds it so funny,
Seeing me sad.

Help me Mummy,
I can't move,
He's shouting at me Mummy,
I'm going to lose.

Mummy please tell a friend,
Mummy make this horror end.

Lucy Simpson (13)
The Hundred of Hoo School, Rochester

Time To Change

The pollution in the air,
That will extinguish the bear,
Because of the motorways and the cars,
The cafés and the bars.

Recycle here, recycle there,
That will save the bear,
As the sea levels rise,
People see it as a surprise.

Hotter and hotter it will get,
It is making people sweat.

It is time to change,
Before the Earth starts to look strange.

Joshua Sparks (13)
The Hundred of Hoo School, Rochester

She Hurt Me

I used to think that others
Didn't have mothers
Who were as cruel as mine.

As each day went past
I thought about how long
This awful pain could last.

But I stood tall,
Throughout it all,
Even though she hurt me.

Soon I found the strength
To tell someone,
About the great lengths
My mum went through,
To hurt me.

Sadie Payne (13)
The Hundred of Hoo School, Rochester

Mask

I sit and wonder what life's all about
A world full of destruction with no meaning.
I crave for someone to listen, someone to hear,
But I walk away with loneliness and fear
I put on a mask to show the world I am not scared
But in reality I am in tears
Without the mask I am nobody
With nothing but a heart to give
To be noticed
I pray to overcome all this,
I pray with all my heart
To wake from this nightmare
With no hurt . . . no mask.

Eleanor Cox (14)
The Hundred of Hoo School, Rochester

Bullies

Let's fight
Let's all unite.
Let's punch
And rob the bully's lunch.
Let's kick
And hit the bullies with the stick.
Stand up tall,
Don't let them knock you down.
Smile, don't let them
Make you frown.
Feel up, don't let
Them make you feel down.
Humiliate the bullies,
Make them look
Like clowns.

Taylor Warrington (12)
The Hundred of Hoo School, Rochester

Help Me

Every night I lay here still,
Hoping someone will come
Everyone's around me
But no one ventures near.

All the bruises and sores
Never seem to go,
My mum says to go
But my heart says *no!*

I thought he would go soon,
Turned out I was wrong,
Finally he left
And my life wasn't a mess.

Megan Moseley (12)
The Hundred of Hoo School, Rochester

And They All Lived Happily Ever After

I feel so small
When he strolls to me
He's oh so tall
Please don't hit me

Ring! Ring! Ring! Oh please no,
Text message states, 'R.I.P Sid'
I strolled to Asda and co
And there he is

On Tuesday I had 50 pence
I met Max he had a lot of lip
But I had confidence
And friendship.

James Bullen (13)
The Hundred of Hoo School, Rochester

My Terrible Life

I used to be so scared,
When I got home from school,
It seemed like no one cared,
How could he be so cruel?

Then I told someone,
I felt scared inside,
How he thought it was fun,
How he made me cry.

If the same has happened to you,
And you're not sure what to do,
Don't make the same mistake,
Tell someone before it's too late.

Paige Maguire (13)
The Hundred of Hoo School, Rochester

Abuse

'Daddy don't do it!'
My daddy comes thundering in
He squares up to me, and gives me a hit
Mummy comes in and saves the day!

'Daddy please stop it!'
Every single day I need to give him pay
Just to stop him from having a fit
But Mummy saves the day!

'Daddy I need it!'
My daddy lost his phone
He takes mine away when I need it
But Mummy always saves the day!

Sam Ridgewell (13)
The Hundred of Hoo School, Rochester

Change The World

If I could change the world,
This is what I would do;
I would change racism and bullying.
These are sad things and people say
That you are a coward if you do so.
People can get bullied about anything,
Colour of their skin,
Fat or thin or being dyslexic.
It is not their fault for being who they are.
Why don't people accept that?

Summer Chapman (13)
The Hundred of Hoo School, Rochester

War

Civil blood
Love hate
Guns
Bang
Life and death
Vietnam's victims
Hitler's holocaust
One man gone
Millions more to come.
Bang, boom, bomb!

Blair Robb (14)
The Hundred of Hoo School, Rochester

I Want To Change

I want to change the world to a much better place.
To reunite countries and make just one race
I would like to stop war and make guns into sweets.
To help the African generation live to eat.

Stop poverty, cure illness, that's our aim
To stop child abuse and bullying, the endless game.
Stop domestic violence, what's the point of it?
Women and young girls being viciously hit.

Georgie Wright, Robyn Danquah, Harry & Jake Perkins (14)
The Hundred of Hoo School, Rochester

Don't Like Mondays

Don't like Mondays
Wish we had more fun days
Don't like early mornings,
Can hear more sleep calling.
Don't like rainy days,
If only there was more sunny haze,
Don't like school
I hope they do away with the rules.

Matt Chawner (13)
The Hundred of Hoo School, Rochester

I Hear You

I hear your words in my ear
So I know that you are near.
I feel your soul here and there
So my heart I will share.
I see your face all around
So I say I will be proud.
I hear you, I hear you
I miss you.

Hannah Williams (12)
The Hundred of Hoo School, Rochester

I Had A Dream

I was running
Away from death,
Heart thumping with fear,
My death near,
Praying with my last breath,

Creatures closing in,
With swords of evil,
I had nothing,
Just the good in me,

Hissing arrows,
Coming closer,
My life near to end,

My heart gave in,
I could not control this world I was in,
Life sapped from my body,
Blood pouring,

Yet good in me kept me going,
Until the last . . . br . . . ea . . . th . . .

Christian Horn (13)
The Oratory School, Reading

I Have A Dream

I have a dream to go back in time,
I have a dream that one day I'll fly.
I have a dream that I'll live forever,
I have a dream that we'll end up together.

I had a dream we met up as kids,
I had a dream that we travelled the world.
I had a dream we married each other,
And I believed,
We were perfect for each other.

But dreams are dreamt and they don't come true,
But in life try and try until they do.
You should dream your dream as if it will last forever,
However live your life as you'll never, never
. . . live again.

Really forever doesn't exist,
And forever is just a string of nows.
And if you want now to last forever.
Then just remember,
To forget about the now that's just been
And don't worry about the now that's about to be.
Just concentrate on the now that's at the moment,
And dream that life will become an agreement.

However I've dreamt and dreamt my life will come good
And my dreams will come true.
But just in case
Things don't fall into place
I've lived life with a smile on my face.

Conor Jones (14)
The Oratory School, Reading

I Have A Dream . . .

I have a dream
That just one day
Happiness will come
And never go away.
That people will come
Together in drones,
Without bored sighs,
Without bored moans,
And men and women
All over this land,
Will come together
Hand in hand,
And maybe then
A few will dance,
Some could skip,
Some could prance.

But is this far
Or is this near?
The details still remain unclear,
But of course
The of course
The dream lives on
Forever and ever
On and on.

Henry Cope (14)
The Oratory School, Reading

I Have A Dream

Sitting, thinking, wondering with nothing but
The roosters chanting their daily morning ritual,
The performance of the birds enlightening,
With the silence of the park images, thoughts come wailing in,
A day on the moon,
A home underwater,
Being able to fly,
Each image I imagine with precision,
I begin to wonder *have I been here before*
Is this déjá vu?

Returning when the owls' kingdom is at its midst,
Again silence, but not the same,
The twittering of the owls almost unnerving,
Streams of colliding delineation merging into horror,
A sudden chill,
A fear,
Noises in my head play tricks,
I see things never seen before,
Creatures and beasts,
Rustles come from every direction,
Trees turn to graves,
And benches turn into bodies,
And I listen to my conscious, *run!*

Fin Johnson (14)
The Oratory School, Reading

I Have A Nightmare

Once I had a nightmare
It wasn't very nice
All full of cloud
And freezing pain, on cold, bleak fields of ice
It corresponds, quite well in fact
To our current state of play
Where cynical wars cover all
And nature's torn asunder
Where has it gone, our simple decent manner?
To give way to a corporate shell
An iron skeleton that speaks no words
But numbered code, for bombs, buildings of sin
'The military shall rule the world'
So proudly preached the leader
With brute-like force, emotions gone
The children are made ready to fight the battle of the damned
Lay down a life before it has begun
But then broke through a ray of hope
My nightmares are now dreams
That ray of hope I trust to come
Quite soon in real life
It could be me, or you, or us
Let's only hope it comes on time, not late.

Alexander Frank (12)
The Oratory School, Reading

Like A Dream

Dreams are wondrous, extravagant and strange,
They make you think in all different ways.
They separate the night from the day
But just hope you can keep the nightmares at bay.
Dreams are a different world when you are asleep.
But when you're awake they can make you weep.
Dreams can conjure different emotions
Your brain still awake whilst you are asleep.
All this in the night can make you feel rotten
But by the morning the dreams are all forgotten.
My dreams are like a different life inside my head
That keep my brain occupied as I go to bed.
Some people dream about horrible things
Like wars and dead brothers
But people with no worries
Are awoken from them by their mothers.

Oscar Chandler (13)
The Oratory School, Reading

I Had A Dream

I've always wanted to be dead,
To wander round without a head,
Escape from all my sorrows past,
And wake up wholly dead at last.

I lay awake within my bed,
Wondering what it would be like if I were dead,
But I'm so startled by what I see,
The death I see is surely me.

I curl up small within my bed,
I really don't want to be dead,
The pain I see that it would cause
Has put my longing for death on pause.

Horatio Carr-Jones (14)
The Oratory School, Reading

What Do You Dream About?

Racing cars, super spies,
Chocolate sundaes and massive pies!
Winning gold
Being bold
Gleaming bikes
Brand new Nikes
Scoring the goal
Coming in to bowl
Taking the wicket
That's the ticket!
Fancy new shoes
A five star cruise
Becoming a prince
Being rich ever since
Getting loads of money
Visited by the Easter bunny
Licking an ice cream
What a cracking dream!

Charlie Dunn (14)
The Oratory School, Reading

My Dream

As I lay, in silence and peace,
I dreamt of the perfect world,
One with no hatred, only love,
No wars or suffering,
But the safety all people look for,
Some look to family and friends
And many turn their heads to the sky,

In this perfect world neither religion nor race
Would cause war or suffering.
But how can this perfect world be made,
We must dream, as for many dreams are all we have.

Charlie Martin (14)
The Oratory School, Reading

I Have A Dream

What dream do you have
A leader of the people changing the world
The power of one man's voice striking above all the rest
With words of force and meaning?

The dream of a different world conjured up in my thoughts
The power that you were imagining you had.
The things you could do to make the world a world of hope.
The things you could say to make people smile with pleasure.
Your voice, the most powerful thing in my body.

The dream of stopping wars with just a single word.
The dream of us all being like birds
Or the dream that has no purpose but to make you smile?

Do you have demons and fear in your nightmares
Or do you conquer them with a flash of your sword
Or a bullet in your gun?
So what are the dreams that you have-
Hope and pleasure
Or war and fear?

Charlie Baker (15)
The Oratory School, Reading

Harmony

I have a dream,
That one day people will live in peace,
That Man will have nothing to fear,
That all fighting and war will cease,
And the world, but a peaceful sphere

I have a dream,
That no-mans-land will be a thing of the past
No gun will have to be fired
No man will have to stand fast
And nothing would be desired.

I have a dream
That everyone will be loved
And everybody will have a reason to live
No animal will be left unloved
And everything will thrive.

Zak Mason (13)
The Oratory School, Reading

The Dream Of War

The pictures flood in,
Swirling into one big mass of undulating colours.
It suddenly becomes clear.
The hammer drops and a sound shakes the images,
Why is there war!
To settle the differences two self-absorbed leaders,
Or to simply entertain their egocentric humours?
When I wake from this dream,
What is there for me?
Just another day that the leaders use me as a pawn,
In their demented game of chess.
When will the killing cease
And the weapons lay down?
That is my dream.

Ollie Butt (14)
The Oratory School, Reading

Midday Dream

On a silent, warm and undisturbed midday,
I lie awake beneath the shaded grove.
Light rays play with the shadows in the air
And colours are reflected from the mirrors back into my face,
The eyes close slowly . . .silent are the surroundings.

On silent, warm and undisturbed midnight,
I lie awake beneath the ancient grove,
The moon shines brightly, warming my pale skin
With the colourful spectre of lights;
Breathe in . . .and out; feel the air going through
Each chamber of your body.

I stand on ancient hill and feel hot rays
Going through my transparent body, I rise . . .
And now I fly beneath those stars and
Touch those constellations with my trembling palm.
I see the light above my head and fly towards it . . .
In front of golden gates I stand . . .

I see angels flying above me; see warm smiles on their faces;
I ask them for directions but they say, 'Go away,'
I look down to the lower world and see the depression and mortality,
Pale-skinned people, like myself, wandering about . . .meaninglessly.
I beg angels to change their mind, but in vain, 'Go away.'

On silent, warm and undisturbed midday,
I wake up beneath the silent grove
The colours disappear . . . it is late.
I stand and see the bright star lonely in the sky.
There is no Heaven, but no pallor and depression around me . . .
I breathe,
I stand and listen to the music of the evening:
Am I asleep or am I awake?

Georgy Filippov (17)
Wellington College, Crowthorne

Land Of The Free

Miss Holbrook called it the Land Of The Free,
and then said that MLK was right, and told me teacherly
about black rights but I didn't care, because firstly
I didn't believe a woman who said *one*
rhymed with *won* 'from sea to shining sea' -
besides, my best friend was white-toothed and Jamaican

Ms Ackerman, eight feet wide and twice as tall,
made me cry for writing *a lot.* Surely I murmur,
a lot of people make mistakes? And I hope wildly
that a teacher who listens to country music and not to you,
and a dead goldfish (a coldfish), and penning in empty spaces,
and crossed-out tear-smudges aren't Freedom.

They say you don't miss something 'til it's gone,
and Miss Harvey certainly didn't, especially
when I was unruly and unsmiley and imperfect, so I'd wait,
shaking under Shakespeare and Dickens, my dusty sentinels -
then she'd sigh, and dissect my last-minute corrections,
my hopeful scribblings, my awkward Stateside spellings.

Hello high school, I love this class but every word I write
seems to inspire . . . anger in English departments. Perhaps
It's because I'm not English? But even so, neither was Frost,
and *he* was brilliant and everybody figures brilliance
is ultimately freedom. Ultimately - and non-believers like me
still believe they'll make you cry, for painting truths across the sky.

Bethan Cotterill (15)
Wellington College, Crowthorne

Missed And Missing

I watch that girl, silly plaits and frock
One hand pointing in the shop
The other held tightly by
A man, who could have stopped her cry

I look at my own and what do I see?
An empty space where a hand should be
And when we sit, there's that empty chair
My father, my father, he should have been there

And when I tripped on something daft
Where was his melting, healing laugh?
Or those times when my brother and I had fought
Where was that teacher that I sought?

It was me who had held his hand
In the sun, my brother I fanned
So he should not feel the sorrow
Our father, the father he would not know

I woke one day, from a sleep so warm
Having dreamed my father's form
Touched his laugh, and heard his smiles:
Conversation enough for miles

The very girl, who stood in the shop
We passed her by but noticed her not
For I was his and his hand mine
Nothing more to make me shine

And when I catch myself alone
I wonder if he should not have gone
Would I have jumped higher or lower fall?
Would I even have changed at all?

Now when my children kneel to pray
Innocent wishes they whisper away
It is then my father's laugh I hear
Listening, laughing, I know he's near.

Swati Parida (17)
Woking College, Woking

Young Writers Information

We hope you have enjoyed reading this book - and that you will continue to enjoy it in the coming years.

If you like reading and writing poetry drop us a line, or give us a call, and we'll send you a free information pack.

Alternatively if you would like to order further copies of this book or any of our other titles, then please give us a call or log onto our website at www.youngwriters.co.uk

Young Writers Information
Remus House
Coltsfoot Drive
Peterborough
PE2 9JX
(01733) 890066